ARNOLD SCHOENBERG

MODERN MASTERS

MODERN MASTERS

EDITED BY frank kermode

arnold schoenberg

charles rosen

NEW YORK | THE VIKING PRESS

First published in 1975 in a hardbound and a paperbound
edition by
The Viking Press, Inc., 625 Madison Avenue,
New York, N.Y. 10022

LIBRARY OF CONGRESS CATALOGING IN PUBLICATION DATA

Rosen, Charles, 1927–
Arnold Schoenberg.

(Modern masters ; M29)
Bibliography: p.
Includes index.

1. Schönberg, Arnold, 1874–1951.
ML410.S283R65   780′.92′4   72–78996
ISBN 0–670–13316–7
ISBN 0–670–01986–0 pbk.

Printed in U.S.A.

Chapter i, under the title "The Controversial Schoenberg,"
originally appeared in the September 1974 issue of *High
Fidelity*. Chapter ii originally appeared in the Spring 1975
issue of *Georgia Review*.

TO LISL

PREFACE

Schoenberg thought of himself as an inevitable historical force. Once when asked if he was the famous composer Arnold Schoenberg, he replied, "No one else
wanted the job, so I had to take it on." He became a
classic without ever winning the ungrudging public acceptance granted to lesser figures. The permanence of
his achievement is now secure, the weight of his influence recognized: their significance, however, remains
the subject of controversy.

Today we are no longer under any obligation to per-
suade listeners of his importance, or even to assess it; but
his work cannot be characterized without accounting for
the resistance it aroused. Schoenberg's achievement appears to many musicians as an uneven one, but it has
seemed to me of very little interest to say which works I
like best and which I think least successful. In any case,
that will be perfectly clear in what follows; but the exer-

cise of taste for its own sake makes for dubious criticism: it is more valuable to suggest the terms of a discussion in which various and even conflicting judgments may reasonably be argued. Evaluation is more cogent and convincing as a by-product than as a goal or even a starting point of criticism.

Of the many people who have helped me with this short account of Schoenberg, I should like most of all to thank Elliott Carter, who generously lent me books, scores, tapes, and records, and who made many invaluable points. Henri Zerner persuaded me to excise some nonsense in the first two chapters and made many stylistic improvements. I am also indebted to Frank Kermode for the suggestions he made with great kindness when I was putting the completed manuscript into shape. Elisabeth Sifton expects her aid and her helpful, sympathetic editing to be taken for granted, but I am very grateful for them nonetheless.

C.R.

CONTENTS

Supposing times were normal—normal as they were before 1914—then the music of our time would be in a different situation.

—ARNOLD SCHOENBERG, 1936

BIOGRAPHICAL NOTE

1874   Arnold Schoenberg born September 13.

1882   Began to study the violin and to compose.

1898   Performance of a String Quartet in D major at the Vienna Tonkünstlerverein (first work to be played in public).

1899   Composed Sextet, *Verklaerte Nacht*, op. 4.

1900–01 Composed the *Gurrelieder*.

1901   Moved to Berlin.

1902–03 Composed *Pelleas und Melisande,* op. 5, tone poem.

1903   Returned to Vienna.

1904–05 String Quartet no. 1 in D minor, op. 7.

1906   Chamber Symphony no. 1, op. 9.

1907–08 String Quartet no. 2 in F-sharp minor, op. 10.

1909   Three Piano Pieces, op. 11.

        Das Buch der Hängenden Gärten, op. 15, songs to poems by Stefan George.

        Five Pieces for Orchestra, op. 16.

        A one-act opera, *Erwartung,* op. 17.

1911	Moved to Berlin.
	Completed orchestration of the *Gurrelieder*.
	Six Little Pieces for Piano, op. 19.
	Completed the treatise on harmony.
1912	*Pierrot Lunaire*, op. 21, three cycles of seven poems.
1913	First performance of *Gurrelieder*, February 23, Vienna. Great success.
	Riot at performance of music by Webern, Berg, and Schoenberg, March 31.
1915–17	Military service.
1917	Returned to Vienna. Founded the Society for the Private Performance of Music.
1921	Invention of twelve-tone technique.
1923	Completion of Piano Pieces op. 23, Suite for Piano op. 25, Serenade op. 24.
1924	Wind Quintet op. 26.
	Moved to Berlin, professor at the Prussian Academy of Fine Arts.
1926–27	String Quartet no. 3, op. 30.
1928	Variations for Orchestra, op. 31.
1929	One-act opera, *Von Heute auf Morgen*, op. 32.
1930	Music for a Film Sequence, op. 34.
1932	*Moses und Aron*, opera. Two acts finished.
1933–34	Dismissed from post in Berlin. Returned to Jewish faith. Left for the United States and settled in Hollywood, teaching at the University of California.
1936	Violin Concerto op. 36.
	String Quartet no. 4, op. 37.
1942	*Ode to Napoleon*, op. 41.
	Piano Concerto op. 42.
1944	Retired from University of California.
1946	String Trio op. 45.
1947	*Survivor from Warsaw*, op. 46.
1949	Fantasia for Violin and Piano, op. 47.
1951	Died Friday, July 13.

Expressionism

i

In 1945, Arnold Schoenberg's application for a grant was turned down by the Guggenheim Foundation. The hostility of the music committee to Schoenberg and to his work was undisguised. The seventy-year-old composer had hoped for support in order to finish two of his largest musical compositions, the opera *Moses und Aron* and the oratorio *Die Jakobsleiter (Jacob's Ladder)*, as well as several theoretical works. Schoenberg had just retired from the University of California at Los Angeles; since he had been there only eight years, he had a pension of thirty-eight dollars a month with which to support a wife and three children aged thirteen, eight, and four. He was obliged, therefore, to spend much of his time taking private pupils in composition. This enforced teaching enabled him to complete only one of the theoretical works, the *Structural Functions of Harmony*. The opera and oratorio were still unfinished at the composer's death six years later.

Recognized internationally as one of the greatest living composers, considered the finest of all by many, acknowledged, with Igor Stravinsky, as one of the two most influential figures in contemporary music since Debussy, Arnold Schoenberg at the end of his life continued to provoke an enmity, even a hatred, almost unparalleled in the history of music. The elderly artist whose revolutionary works had raised a storm of protest in his youth is a traditional figure, but in old age his fame is generally unquestioned and dissenting voices have been stilled. In Schoenberg's case, the dissent may be said to have grown with the fame.

At the end of his life Schoenberg recognized the importance of the hostility that he had faced throughout his career. In 1947, the National Institute of Arts and Letters gave him a grant of a thousand dollars: this was the award generally made to promising young composers, but the more prestigious one would have aroused an implacable opposition. It is unlikely that Schoenberg knew how he was being slighted; he could be brutally sarcastic when he felt, as he so often did, that he was being denied the honors that were his due, but on this occasion he expressed his gratitude for the award, in a speech that he recorded in his strange English and sent to the National Institute to be played at the meeting. But he also characterized his life in a terrifying and grotesque image: "Personally I had the feeling as if I had fallen into an ocean of boiling waters, and not knowing how to swim or to get out in another manner, I tried with my legs and arms as best I could. . . . I never gave up. But how could I give up in the middle of an ocean?"

And he spoke of his opponents with an inimitable combination of genuine sympathy and equally genuine fury: "It might have been the desire to get rid of this nightmare, of this unharmonious torture, of these unintelligible ideas, of this methodical madness—and I must admit: these were not bad men who felt this way—though of course I never understood what I had done to them to make them as malicious, as furious, as cursing, as aggressive . . ." At the end he paid them a superb tribute in speaking of what he had achieved in his life: "Maybe something has been achieved but it was not I who deserves the credit for that. The credit must be given to my opponents. They were the ones who really helped me." It was as if he saw that the controversial nature of his work was central to its significance.

He had not at first expected controversy, and he did not often, in fact, consciously or openly seek it out. His early works are Brahmsian, even Dvoràkian, in character, solid and unadventurous. Wagner was to become for him a more advanced model, but hardly by the late 1890s a dangerously revolutionary one: yet the Wagnerism of the string sextet *Verklaerte Nacht (Transfigured Night)*, written when Schoenberg was twenty-five, created difficulties. "It sounds as if someone had smeared the score of *Tristan* while it was still wet," remarked a contemporary, and a musical society in Vienna refused to allow the work to be performed because it contained one dissonance (now harmless to our ears) as yet unclassified by any textbook. Already in 1898, the year before *Verklaerte Nacht* was written, there had been a minor disturbance after the performance of one of Schoenberg's songs, and Schoenberg was to recall it many years later and comment, "The scandal has never ceased."

All these early difficulties, however, are the normal ones encountered by most composers in the history of Western music since the Renaissance—and by most writers and artists as well. A unanimous critical success from the very outset has even come to seem somewhat suspicious. It is expected that a new style, a new personality, will have a toughness and individuality bound to excite opposition. The initial opposition, indeed, is an essential ingredient of the later success and turns acceptance into triumph.

In the early part of his career, this success was not withheld from Schoenberg. He gradually won the respect and support of musicians of the importance of Ferruccio Busoni, Richard Strauss, and Gustav Mahler. The critics were beginning to come around. As for the public, the first performance of a new work by Schoenberg was generally followed by a display of hostility—a sort of minor riot which was accepted as a ritual element in Viennese concert life, but second performances were quiet and often successful, even brilliantly so. The tone poem of 1902–1903, *Pelleas und Melisande,* was handsomely received when it was played in Berlin in 1907. Finally in Vienna on February 23, 1913, came an almost unmitigated triumph, with the first performance of the immense *Gurrelieder,* a long work for the gigantic forces of six soloists, four choruses, and an orchestra of a hundred and fifty. Many people came to the first performance ready to whistle on their house keys (the traditional Viennese method of expressing public displeasure), but the house keys were not used: people wept and cheered, and Schoenberg received an ovation that lasted a quarter of an hour.

The triumph of February 23 was, in fact, a posthumous

one, a celebration for a composer who had changed almost beyond recognition. Schoenberg had already traveled far beyond the *Gurrelieder,* which he had written in 1900 and orchestrated only in 1911. The next concert that Schoenberg gave, on March 31, 1913, brought total disaster, a riot even more destructive than that provoked slightly earlier by the first performance in Paris of Stravinsky's *Rite of Spring.* It was not, in fact, Schoenberg's own work that touched off the final uproar (although his Chamber Symphony no. 1, opus 9, had been listened to with growing displeasure), but one by his young pupil Alban Berg: a song to words sent on a picture post card by the Viennese poet Peter Altenberg. The rest of the program had to be canceled and the police called out. Berg himself never recovered from the hostility of this occasion, and he was never to hear a performance of the *Altenberg Lieder.*

Today it is possible to recognize the identity of the composer of the *Gurrelieder* and that of the later works, to see the relation between them and even the gradual development from one to the other, to find the radical change already latent in the early work. But the change was rapid and far-reaching, as Schoenberg himself recognized when, in 1911, while orchestrating the *Gurrelieder,* he tried to alter four or five passages: these corrections alone, he confessed, gave him more trouble than the composition of the whole work. For by the beginning of 1909 the break with the style of 1901 was already almost complete. If the works of Schoenberg's pupils Alban Berg and Anton Webern, played at that catastrophic occasion of March 31, 1913, were far more radical than the Chamber Symphony of their teacher, that is because Schoenberg had cautiously withheld his most recent works (the Chamber Symphony dated from 1906).

The presence of works of Berg and Webern also underlines the fact that this development of Schoenberg had not taken place in solitude. He had found in the much younger Webern and Berg genius equal to his own, and of an even more remarkable precocity. It is clear that the most radical experiments were initiated by Schoenberg himself, and both Webern and Berg considered themselves his disciples, but the influence soon became reciprocal, and Schoenberg owed much to the stimulation of his pupils. What is remarkable is the rapidity with which both Webern and Berg adopted the most thoroughgoing innovations of their teacher, the ease with which ideas only suggested in Schoenberg's music were developed by them in the most individual way. Particularly for the years 1906–1914 there was a genuine and almost absolute community of spirit. It may be conjectured that without the extraordinary support and understanding of his two greatest pupils, Schoenberg might not have been able to overcome his own resistance to the revolution he was initiating.

Schoenberg himself acknowledged this resistance, essential to an understanding of the character of his music and of his later development. It was with more than reluctance that Schoenberg embarked on the series of works that begin with the *George-Lieder* of 1909, as he himself admitted in the notes to the first performance on January 14, 1910:

> With the *George* songs I have for the first time succeeded in approaching an ideal of expression and form which has been in my mind for years. Until now, I lacked the strength and confidence to make it a reality. But now that I am conscious of having broken through every restriction of a bygone aesthetic; and though the goal toward which I am striving appears to me a cer-

tain one, I am, nonetheless, already feeling the resistance I shall have to overcome; I feel now how hotly even the least of temperaments will rise in revolt, and suspect that even those who have so far believed in me will not want to acknowledge the necessary nature of this development. . . . I am being forced in this direction. . . . I am obeying an inner compulsion which is stronger than any upbringing.[1]

To speak of an inner compulsion is to recognize one's own unwillingness to yield, to feel the weight of the opposition and even partially to admit its validity.

In his justification, Schoenberg brings forward the classic dichotomy of nature and civilization, the opposition of an inner compulsion and an "artistic education" (as he later characterizes "upbringing"). In this notorious pair, the rights are traditionally on the side of nature —and, indeed, Schoenberg's critics were to accuse him of violating the natural laws of music, of substituting a purely artificial system for one that had been handed down to be used along with the laws of physics. Nature has generally been the ground upon which to build any aesthetic theory, and the most contradictory positions have claimed a base there. If the dichotomy of nature and art can so easily be stood on its head, it should lead us to be suspicious of the opposition. A great deal of nonsense has been written about the relation of music to the laws of acoustics or even to the configuration of the human ear, but the irresistible force of history—essentially the same thing as Schoenberg's "inner compulsion"—ought not to inspire greater confidence in any of its simpler forms. The resistance to Schoenberg's radical break with the nineteenth-century tradition was as

[1]Cited in Willi Reich, *Schoenberg,* p. 49.

inevitable as the break itself, and this resistance, as we shall see, is reflected in the music itself.

What should be emphasized here is the sense of scandal, the consciousness of moral outrage aroused by Schoenberg's work after 1908, as by all the important artistic achievements of the period. The style of Schoenberg, however—and, indeed, of most of the avant-garde movements of the first decades of this century—was not created solely with an intent to shock. The artists, Schoenberg as much as any, were above all aware of taking the next reasonable and logical step, of doing work that was already to hand and that had to be done. To a certain extent, the stylistic revolutions of those years were merely the exploitation of already existent possibilities within the artistic languages, the drawing of unavoidable conclusions. Nevertheless, the sense of rebellion cannot be easily dismissed. Much of the music and art of that period is deliberately provocative and expresses a defiance, even a profound horror, of the society in which the artists lived.

Throughout the nineteenth century, the resistance of the general public to new artistic movements had grown steadily. A fear of what is original and difficult to comprehend is no doubt a constant in history, but the accelerated rate of stylistic change after 1800 and the rapid expansion of the mass public interested in consuming art combined to make the normally difficult relation between artist and public a pathological one. The artist and his public each conceived the other as a threat. The artist's answer to ideological pressure was one of deliberate provocation, while the public came to believe that a violent response to such provocation was a citizen's right and even a patriotic duty. A conservative taste in art seemed to many the last defense against anarchy. By the end of the century, the works of poets as different as Mallarmé, Jarry, and George express a powerful contempt for the public, and this contempt veils an even more profound hatred.

Nowhere was this hatred more open than in Vienna: if the pastime of shocking the bourgeois took on at times a playful aspect in Paris and London, in Vienna it was carried on with a bitter seriousness only occasionally masked by wit. Adolf Loos (with Peter Behrens the greatest of central Europe's architects of the first decade of the twentieth century) founded a review with the characteristically insulting title *The Other, a Paper for the Introduction of Western Culture into Austria*.

The conservative taste in music of the Viennese public was the most uncompromising in Europe. The existence and integrity of what was locally felt to be the greatest tradition of Western music was menaced by every new step taken, starting with the works of Mahler and even before. By 1910 a concert of contemporary music was an open invitation to a hostile demonstration. The more hospitable artistic atmosphere of Paris (where they took music less seriously) was not to be found in Vienna. Furthermore, Paris had a tradition of artistic rebellion which was firmly established and accepted as a counterculture, and which the artists of central Europe looked at with envy and tried to imitate in vain before the limited and fragile success of Berlin in the 1920s. But for the Viennese artist and musician, the public was the enemy. When Schoenberg in 1911 was given a minor post at the Vienna Royal Academy of Music, largely on Mahler's recommendation, this was the signal for a public protest in the Austrian Parliament, where a member challenged the government to justify such an appointment. When Schoenberg refused the position and moved to Berlin, he wrote firmly, "I wish to say explicitly that I would not come to Vienna even if you were to double the salary. . . . For the present, I could not live in Vienna. I have not yet got over the things done to me there."

The extent to which Schoenberg partially and unconsciously courted the scandal provoked by his work may be measured by one detail. Born in a Jewish family in 1874 but brought up a Catholic, he converted to Protestantism at the age of eighteen. There is no question that the conversion was deeply sincere, but becoming a Protestant in Catholic, imperial Vienna was asking for trouble. (Upon the accession of Hitler to power, in 1933, Schoenberg returned to the Jewish faith.) Nevertheless, the Schoenberg scandal is not merely personal, but part of a much larger historical complex on an international scale, which includes not only the violent reactions to the first performances of Strauss's *Salome* and *Electra* and Stravinsky's *Rite of Spring,* but the sense of direct affront in the exhibition of *Les Fauves* at the *Salon d'Automne* of 1906 (when the work of Matisse, Derain, and Vlaminck was described in the words of Ruskin about Whistler: "a pot of paint flung in the public's face"), the shock created in 1908 by Picasso's whores in the *Demoiselles d'Avignon,* and the morbidity and violence of German expressionist drama and painting.

The interdependence of all these movements is obvious, and, indeed, the identity of the French Fauvist movement and German expressionism was proclaimed by the German expressionists themselves. "Who are the German wild beasts [Fauves]?" wrote Franz Marc in 1912 in *Der Blaue Reiter (The Blue Rider),* the great document of German expressionism. "The majority of them is well known and much written about: the Dresden 'Brücke' [Ernst Ludwig Kirchner, Emil Nolde, Max Pechstein, etcetera], the Berlin Neue Sezession [largely recruited from the Brücke], and the Munich Neue Vereinigung [which became the Blue Rider group of Paul Klee, Vasily Kandinsky, August Macke, and Marc himself]." *The Blue Rider* printed reproductions of the new cubist works of Picasso and Robert Delaunay, numerous works of Henri Rousseau, and two of the greatest of Matisse's paintings, *La Musique* and *La Danse*. There are almost as many articles on music in *The Blue Rider* as on painting, including an essay by Schoenberg and a discussion of the music of Skryabin. Songs by Webern and Berg were also included, along with a facsimile of the manuscripts of Schoenberg's *Herzgewächse* for soprano, celeste, harmonium, and harp. For a number of years Schoenberg thought of himself as a painter as well as a composer; his paintings were exhibited in the Blue Rider exhibition of 1912, and two were reproduced in *The Blue Rider* itself. The paintings, admired by Kandinsky among others, are seen today as an interesting marginal phenomenon, like Goethe's watercolors or Victor Hugo's wash drawings. But it is in this atmosphere that the music of Schoenberg was created, and it was both inspired by the movements in the other arts and an example to them in its revolutionary boldness.

These movements were all conceived as liberations from the constraint of nature as well as of tradition. "Fauvism came into being," Matisse said, "because we suddenly wanted to abandon the imitation of the local colors of nature and sought by experimenting with pure color to obtain increasingly powerful—obviously instantaneous—effects, and also to achieve greater luminosity." The release from "an imitation of the exterior forms of nature" was also demanded by the expressionists: "it has no significance," Kandinsky wrote in 1912, "whether the artist uses a real or an abstract form. Both are inwardly equal." The revolution of Schoenberg has been described, not least by Schoenberg himself, as "an emancipation of the dissonance." The argument still rages as to whether tonality (like perspective) is a natural or conventional system, but in any case the artistic upheavals of the earlier twentieth century are felt as a new freedom as much from natural as from conventional laws.

The achievement of Schoenberg and his school between the years 1908 and 1913 is still so explosive in its implications that we are only beginning to understand it today. These years saw the creation of many of the greatest works of the school, including most of Webern's best-known works and Berg's Three Pieces for Orchestra and the *Altenberg Lieder.* In a single year, 1909, Schoenberg finished *Das Buch der Hängenden Gärten* (the *Book of the Hanging Garden)*—a song cycle on poems by Stefan George, which he had begun the year before—and wrote the piano pieces, opus 11; the Five Pieces for Orchestra; and the one-act opera *Erwartung.* (The last-named work was completed in seventeen days; Schoenberg wrote it, as he wrote almost everything, in a fury of inspiration. Once he lost the thread of a piece, he could almost never pick it up again without disaster.) In 1911 came *Herzgewächse* and the Six Little Pieces for Piano, opus 19, and in 1912 what was to be his most famous work, *Pierrot Lunaire.* Between 1910 and 1913 he composed the drama with music, *Die Glückliche Hand.* The war put a stop to this extraordinary creative activity, and he was able to write only the Four Songs for Orchestra between 1913 and 1916. Then—as far as publication was concerned—there was silence for many years, and Schoenberg was able to finish nothing more until 1923.

It is the works written between 1908 and 1913 that are

the real basis for the Schoenberg "scandal." An early piece like *Verklaerte Nacht* was easily absorbed into the repertory; only the immense size of the forces required to perform the *Gurrelieder* has prevented similar acceptance. The later works, composed after the invention of serialism in 1921, have, in a strange way, become a normal part of today's music; they are not often heard, but they are the works that have been imitated by hundreds of composers over the world. The later Schoenberg became a model followed so many times that we hear him most often without being aware of it. But the works from 1908–1913, the great expressionist period, remain an achievement that we have not yet come to terms with. Only in Berg's *Wozzeck,* written many years later, do we find the style of this period made more acceptable to us, tempered by Berg's lyricism and dramatic power, more diffuse than the fierce and laconic productions of the prewar period.

The ambience in which these works were created and which they still evoke has an old-fashioned air today. In their intense and morbid expressivity they seem to breathe the stuffy atmosphere of that enclosed nightmare world of expressionist German art in the decade before 1914. Even the wit and the gaiety are macabre; against a background of controlled hysteria, the moments of repose take on an air of death. The texts of *Erwartung* and *Pierrot Lunaire* are no longer satisfactory as literature; to approach these works, we need a sympathy for the period in which they were written (or at the least a suspension of distaste). The poems of George in the settings of both Webern and Schoenberg assume a somber turbulence that is only vaguely hinted at in the original. Like the paintings of Pechstein and the poetry of Georg Trakl and Georg Heym, the stylistic language is bound up in a complex way with a violent emotional content, and in the end with an implacably hostile view of the exterior world. It would be fatuous to treat morbidity as an artistic defect, but only a blindly formalist view would refuse to recognize its importance at certain historical moments.

Nevertheless, a wholehearted acceptance of the overblown, period hysteria which came as naturally to these artists as a classical reference did to an eighteenth-century poet poses an interesting problem: the relation of the style to the violence of emotion and the harsh philosophy it was used to express. As I have said above, to a great extent the stylistic development of these years in all the arts was not experienced as essentially an ideological one. To all the painters, the new expressionist manner was a development, logical and above all inevitable, from the work of Van Gogh, Cézanne, and Gauguin, and a natural reaction to the new-found beauty in the work of El Greco and to the recently discovered world of African art. The new forms seemed to suggest themselves independently of the ideological significance with which they could be charged (although the artist's acceptance and understanding of these forms were immediately invested with a spiritual significance). Schoenberg, too, believed that his own work arose clearly and naturally out of post-Wagnerian chromaticism and post-Brahmsian asymmetrical phrasing—so clearly, in fact, that the first works must have seemed to the composer if not to his critics to be not at all experimental in character, merely a cautious step along a marked-out path.

Even such timid advances aroused a storm of protest from a conservative musical establishment and a larger public that prided itself on its Pharisaism. The bolder moves were bound to take on the character of an insult to an unworthy public, to express with a defiance that came close to direct provocation the alienation of the artist, an alienation that had changed from a sacred Romantic tradition into an exacerbated and intolerable condition of life. It must be remembered that the artists of that time knew in advance that each step they took, however small, in the only direction they were convinced did not betray their art would inevitably bring them a still greater distance away from their public. It is possible to see today how much of Schoenberg and Strauss is already implicit in Wagner, how far cubism is latent in the paintings of Cézanne (although history is badly represented by such coarse formulations). But insofar as the history of art has a logic, there are moments when the vision of that logic and the drawing of conclusions require the acceptance of a life of insecurity and anguish, and—above all when this new style is conceived in terms of a sincerely personal expression—this anguish appears to be not so much reflected in the art as released through it. The nightmarish anxiety of early-twentieth-century style is as much a part of the artist's life as an expression of the underlying uncertainties of an era. "If only something would happen. . . . This peace is so stinking oily and greasy like glue polish on old furniture," wrote the twenty-three-year-old Georg Heym in 1910, and we do not know whether to treat this as the boredom of an unhappy young poet or the inspiration of a prophet.

It must be acknowledged that the total chromaticism of the music of 1908—like the use of pure bright colors to symbolize feeling—has an adaptability for the representation of extreme emotional states that is more than fortuitous. Most styles have a much wider range than is sometimes realized, and expressionism is not always so lurid and so tormented as it often appears: there are parts of *Pierrot Lunaire* that have lightness and charm, as there are moments of enchanting sweetness throughout Schoenberg's music. But it is easier—or, at any rate, more immediately tempting—to use some styles in one way rather than another: the insistent flow of Wagner's music made the romantic comedy of *Die Meistersinger* more difficult to achieve, more of a *tour de force,* than the vulgar religiosity of *Parsifal;* to convey religious seriousness, on the other hand, Mozart had to turn to an antiquated form like the Baroque contrapuntal chorale prelude in the second act of *The Magic Flute* or to the Handelian fugue in the *Requiem.* The concentrated expressive force of Schoenberg's atonal style is more at ease with the nightmare of the woman in *Erwartung* who dreams she has killed her lover than with the idealist symbolism of *Die Glückliche Hand.*

The career of Richard Strauss is instructive in this respect for both its disinterested courage and its final cowardice. The operas *Salome* and *Electra* that he wrote in 1905 and 1908 are daring in their extreme chromaticism and in their representation of pathological states, but after *Electra* Strauss quickly retreated into eighteenth-century pastiche and the delicious Viennese pastry of *Der Rosenkavalier.*[2] With his retreat came a withdrawal of his support for the more adventurous Schoenberg: "Only a psychiatrist can help poor Schoenberg now. . . . He would do better to shovel snow instead of scribbling on music paper," he wrote in 1913 to Alma

[2]The debt to Mozart, above all to *The Magic Flute,* is above board and has been often remarked. (The least noticed borrowing, however, is the derivation of the entrance of Baron Ochs from the trial by fire and water.)

Mahler, who, with characteristic Viennese tact, let Schoenberg know what was in the letter.[3] Schoenberg's reaction was forthright when, a year later, he was asked to write something for Strauss's fiftieth birthday: "He is no longer of the slightest artistic interest to me, and whatever I may once have learned from him, I am thankful to say I misunderstood."

What had frightened Strauss? It was as if his experiments in chromaticism had led him unknowingly into a brutal world at odds with his more comfortable, solid nature. Was it the grim obscenity of the action of *Salome* and *Electra* that he drew back from, or the prospect implied by the painful dissonance and harsh orchestral color he had called up? Similarly, was Schoenberg led so often to the expression of such poignant, bitter anguish by his extraordinary insight into the potentialities of post-Wagnerian harmony? Or did he go so far in the destruction of the tonal system that had ruled Western music for centuries in the interest of giving form to an anxiety that was part of his public as well as his private universe?

The misunderstanding inherent in these questions—the reason why they ought not to be answered—is that they suggest that a style is a simple vehicle for expressing a meaning or an emotion; they turn the style into a pure form and the emotion into a pure significance. But a form and its meaning cannot be divided so simply, above all in a work of music. The intense relentless expressivity of each moment in a work like *Erwartung* is a formal device as well as an extramusical significance.

[3]Strauss's remarks are as a member of a committee to award the grant of the Mahler Memorial Foundation. His conclusion has a grim humor and a grudging generosity: "Better give him the grant anyway. . . . You can never tell what posterity will say."

There is, in short, no definable difference between the emotional significance of a chord and the formal relationship of the chord to the other notes in the work of music. The ambiguous nightmare symbolism of *Erwartung* is as much a form of expression as its dissonant harmonic structure: the dissonance and the symbolism are related (indeed, often identical), and it is a mistake to think that one *means* or signifies the other.

The music of the early twentieth century, and of Schoenberg in particular, may take a privileged position in any discussion of the significance of the elements of music: during these years, some of the aspects of conveying significance in music are in a pathological state and therefore reveal themselves more clearly through their exaggeration; even the deformations are instructive.

For communication to take place, an assumption, or even a pretense, that the elements of language have a stable meaning must be convincingly maintained, but one cannot assume that any given element of language has a significance or function that is unequivocal, limitable, or definitive. A certain looseness of meaning is necessary, a kind of free play, so that the machinery of language will not grind to a halt. Poetry seizes upon this looseness, upon the possibilities of misunderstanding inherent in language, and creates forms in which the meaning of the elements derives as much (sometimes more) from their place in the individual work as from their use in speech.

Since the eighteenth century, music has offered the traditional model for this process. The vagueness, or the diffuse character, of the meaning conveyed by music has been euphemistically expressed by saying that music is too precise for words. The structures of music are indeed precise, with a kind of beauty and clarity of mathematical proportions that have been the envy of the other arts: the condition for that precision of form is the "vagueness" of significance of the elements and their suppleness, the possibility of their taking on almost any significance within the context of a work. A musical system such as tonality provides a semblance of stability, a way of distinguishing musical sense from nonsense, while allowing that free play of meaning which makes the composer's work possible.

The so-called "breakdown of tonality" at the end of the nineteenth century revealed to what extent this exterior stability was an illusion; more precisely, it was a construction that depended substantially on the individual works of music much more than a linguistic system depends on individual acts of speech. Music is only metaphorically a language; a single work of music may transform and even create an entire musical system, while no act of speech may do more than marginally alter language.

If an individual work of music may alter and even create "language," then the conditions for understanding it must—at least partially—be made evident in the work itself.[4] The process of establishing the conditions

---

[4]This circumspect formulation has an extreme form: i.e., that the work must be comprehensible on the basis of no other knowledge or experience than the work itself, which has sometimes been maintained although it is evidently absurd. The seductiveness of such a theory must arise from the fact that the experience necessary to understand a piece of unfamiliar music is evidently minimal. A radically new work often requires only a few hearings to reach that degree of persuasion that passes in music for understanding, while a work by Dufay or by Mozart is completely intelligible—or at least appears completely intelligible, which is just as satisfactory—to those with little or no knowledge of works by the composer's contemporaries, with no knowledge of the con-

for this intelligibility is as important in Mozart as in Schoenberg. But it is less visible in Mozart, whose work seems to refer to a stable outside system. Each composer, too, both establishes the structure of that system and, in many cases, transcends it by an extraordinarily free play with the elements of music. This free play is easily to be found in Schoenberg, but the explicit reference to an exterior and relatively stable system of meanings has almost vanished. To speak of the "breakdown of tonality" in this connection is to beg the question, as we can see if we look at a similar late-nineteenth-century development in literature. The free play of meaning is also as essential to Montaigne as to Mallarmé—the association of ideas through connotation, etymology, assonance, and rhyme; it is less in evidence in Montaigne because there it is accompanied by a submission to a stable system of discourse that Mallarmé refused to accept. Yet we cannot speak of the breakdown of a linguistic system with Mallarmé, or the decline of French. The "breakdown of tonality" is similarly a fiction.

Between Mozart and Schoenberg, what disappeared was the possibility of using large blocks of prefabricated material in music. The meaning of an element of form in Mozart was given essentially by the structure of each work, but the element was sometimes a large cadential formula lasting many measures. Scales and arpeggios were treated as units, as were a whole range of accompaniment figures. The common language in music was, in essence, the acceptance of such very large units at

temporary "language," in short. The problem that arises from this minimal requirement of historical knowledge in the comprehension of music is one that few historians of music like to contemplate.

certain strategic points—in general, the ends of sections, or cadences.

By the end of the nineteenth century, these blocks of prefabricated material were no longer acceptable to composers with styles as widely variant as Debussy, Schoenberg, and Skryabin. To employ these blocks of material resulted immediately in pastiche: giving them up, however, led to a kind of panic. It seemed as if music now had to be written note by note; only chains of chromatic or whole-tone scales were possible, and these only sparingly. The renunciation of the symmetrical use of blocks of elements in working out musical proportions placed the weight on the smallest units, single intervals, short motifs.

The expressive values of these tiny elements therefore took on an inordinate significance; they replaced syntax. These expressive values were, however, derived directly from tonal music. And since they took a preponderant role in composition it was obvious that a composer would choose elements with the most powerful, even the most violent, values, as these small elements now had to do the work of much larger groups. The relation between the violence and morbidity of emotional expression and the formal changes of style is therefore not fortuitous. The structures that were most successful between 1908 and 1913—for Stravinsky as well as for the "Second Viennese School"—were those that made the greatest use of the intervals most dissonant in traditional tonal terms: the minor second, the seventh, the tritone (or augmented fourth). In his sometimes obsessive and almost despairing reliance on the traditional expressive values to create works of music during this great period, Schoenberg was paradoxically more dependent on an exterior system, on a hidden assumption of a "common language," than Mozart, whose music does not refer to but *conveys* a traditional system of meaning while it creates a new one. In the end, this quality of bearing its own meaning with little reference outside itself probably cannot be denied to Schoenberg's works any more than to Mozart's (although some parts of the mechanism created for this purpose were subject to unusual strain). It is useful, nevertheless, to perpetuate the theory of the breakdown of tonality already current among Schoenberg's contemporaries, including Debussy, as Schoenberg's music is most simply understood against this background of tradition, even if that background was to be wiped out or re-created in very different ways.

The label "expressionist style" ought to suggest that the expressive values of the stylistic elements were being asked to play a central structural role, one that stretched their capabilities unmercifully. In order to assess the historical development and the meaning of Schoenberg's work we must start by trying to ascertain how these expressive values were determined. In other words, what is the system or the context within which these expressive values can function and be assigned a coherent meaning? To do this, we must, at least in a primitive way, try to reconstruct the sense of crisis in music (and the other arts) during the early years of this century, and to make Schoenberg's first revolutionary achievement seem as reasonable and as inevitable as it did to him and to his disciples. The second revolution that Schoenberg engineered in the 1920s had a very different character and influence, but it, too, seemed to grow naturally out of the first, the so-called "emancipation of the dissonance."

Atonality

ii

The primary means of musical expression is dissonance. This is true at least for Western music since the Renaissance. There are secondary factors, of course—rhythm, tone color, accent—but they are all subordinate to dissonance and to some extent dependent on it. (In other musical cultures, these secondary elements may be the basis for musical expression, but this is a question that must be left open here: if we are forced to eliminate some form of dissonance as essential to music, then we may need a thoroughgoing redefinition of the concept "expression.")

There are two general misconceptions about dissonance in music: the first is that a dissonance is a disagreeable noise; the second, that in order for a dissonance to exist at least two notes must be played together. Both of these must be cleared away in order to see in what sense and to what extent the stylistic revolution of the first decades of this century may be described as an emancipation of the dissonance.

There is nothing inherently unpleasant or nasty about a dissonance: insofar as any chord can be said to be beautiful outside of the context of a specific work of music, some of the most mellifluous are dissonances. They are even to most ears more attractive than consonances, although in one respect less satisfying: they cannot be used to end a piece or even a phrase (except, of course, if one wants to make an unusual effect of something incomplete, broken off in the middle).

It is precisely this effect of ending, this cadential function, that defines a consonance. A dissonance is any musical sound that must be resolved, i.e., followed by a consonance: a consonance is a musical sound that needs no resolution, that can act as the final note, that rounds off a cadence. Which sounds are to be consonances is determined at a given historical moment by the prevailing musical style, and consonances have varied radically according to the musical system developed in each culture. Thirds and sixths have been consonances since the fourteenth century; before that they were considered unequivocally dissonant. Fourths, on the other hand, used to be as consonant as fifths: in music from the Renaissance until the twentieth century, they are dissonances. By the fifteenth century, fourths had become an object of theoretical distress: the harmonic system—defined above all by the relation of consonance to dissonance—was changing, and the ancient, traditional classification of fourths as consonances could no longer be maintained. It is not, therefore, the human ear or nervous system that decides what is a dissonance, unless we are to assume a physiological change between the thirteenth and fifteenth century. A dissonance is defined by its role in the musical "language," as it makes possible the movement from tension to resolution which is at the heart of what may be generally called expressivity.[1]

The movement from dissonance to consonance is governed by procedures that constitute the laws of harmony (which are like grammatical rules, and not laws of nature). These do not apply only to music with several voices: a simple unaccompanied melody has the same movement from tension to resolution that we find in a more complex piece. (Once again, I am not here considering non-Western musical systems.) The concept of dissonance must be applied not only to notes that are sung or played together but also to those which succeed each other in time. The notes of a melody can be dissonant or consonant to each other.

It is by this means that a melody can imply its own harmony, as most tunes in fact do. The themes of Bach, it has often been observed, supply their own bass and very often some of the middle voices as well. Harmony is not a natural attribute of sound but a way of giving significance to sound.[2] To a culture such as ours, which

[1] I am here making a fallacious identification of "expression" and "expressivity," but the fallacy lies in the very center of European music since the sixteenth-century madrigal.

[2] Harmony is, of course, based on some of the natural acoustic attributes of sound, but they are carefully selected, some musical systems leaving out—or even deforming—attributes basic to others. A simple melody that may be expressive in one musical language is merely unintelligible or cacophonous in another. It must be emphasized that the expressive character of music is *neither an inherent acoustic quality of the sound nor a conventional sign that we must learn as we learn the meaning of a word.* It is a derivation from the harmonic system of our culture; the rules of harmony and counterpoint (which are, in fact,

refuses to understand music outside a harmonic context, melodies will naturally be composed that imply this necessary context. A note in a single monophonic line that moves toward resolution within the frame of meaning provided by the melody as a whole is dissonant, and it is from this relation between tension and resolution that an unaccompanied melody derives most of its expressive character.

In this continuous swing between tension and resolution, the complete "emancipation of the dissonance" meant, and could only have meant, a freedom from consonance, from the obligation to resolve the dissonance. It was not merely that any combination of notes was to be admitted, but there was to be no longer any necessity to follow a dissonant chord with a consonance. By 1908 Schoenberg demanded not only the full chromatic complexity that other composers such as Skryabin and Strauss had already won, but even more: a release from the basic harmonic conception of the cadence, the movement toward release of tension, toward absolute repose, which had been fundamental to centuries of music. From this refusal of resolution comes the aptness of the style of the Schoenberg of 1908 to 1914 for the representation of anguish and the macabre.

But if dissonance is understood as that which demands resolution (and this definition must be maintained if the expressive role of dissonance in the language of musical representation is to be understood), if it has meaning only as part of an opposition consonance-dissonance, then the elimination of consonance, of resolution, destroys the basis for expression, makes dissonance itself

---

identical) govern, as we have seen, not just polyphonic music but the successive notes of a melody.

meaningless. The powerful emotional force of Schoen-berg's music would then become intelligible only against an inherited background of traditional harmony, and would itself be an incoherent system, dependent on a musical culture it was intent on destroying.

To put it this way is to neglect the way the operations of dissonance and consonance are re-created and refor-mulated in Schoenberg's music, as in that of Berg and Webern. Every new style seems at once to make non-sense of the preceding one, and yet to retain part of it selectively as essential to its own operations. Chopin's music, for example, was as destructive of the tonic-domi-nant polarization of eighteenth-century style as Schoen-berg's of late-nineteenth-century chromaticism. But the elements of the previous style that are necessary to the understanding and effectiveness of the new one are rein-stated by the new style itself; a style is not so much a language as a way of interpreting a language, and it must offer the conditions and the means for interpreta-tion. The achievement of Schoenberg must be seen against the history of the expansion of dissonance from a simple interval or chord to a large-scale structural de-vice. The "emancipation of the dissonance" was part of a much wider phenomenon: the end of the long, gradual breakdown of tonality.

Tonality is not, as is sometimes claimed, a system with a central note but one with a central perfect triad:[3] all the other triads, major and minor, are arranged around the

[3]The perfect triads are those based upon the primary overtones of a note (for example, on C, the triad is C–E–G). Nontriadic systems with a central note are generally given some name other than "tonal," the most usual being "modal": even this has disadvantages, as a mode, at least in Western music, is defined not only by a central note but by a range and a set of cadential formulas.

central one in a hierarchical order. The central triad, called the tonic, determines the key of the individual piece of music. The distance of the other triads from the tonic is a relation of *dissonance*—their place in the hierarchy defines how far away they are from a final resolution. A tonal work must begin by implying the central position of the tonic, and it must end with it;[4] therefore everything that follows the opening and precedes the final tonic may be conceived as dissonant in relation to the tonic triad, the only perfect consonance.[5]

A pretonal piece in Western music (a modal piece) does not have to end with a triad but only with a central note, the note of the mode; to this note a fifth or an octave could be added. Dissonance was conceived exclusively in terms of intervals. When music became triadic in nature, a new and powerful concept of expression was added: to the idea of the dissonant interval was joined the idea of the dissonant phrase or the dissonant section. *Modulation* is the name given to this process: it is the setting up of a second triad as a sort of polarized force or antitonic against the tonic; the second triad functions as a subsidiary tonic in that part of the piece where it holds

[4]There are a number of works of Romantic and late Romantic music in which these rules are broken: this is a special stylistic effect similar to an anacoluthon, and to be understood requires that the rules are not only taken for granted but implied by the music itself.

[5]There is a weak sense of "tonality" sometimes found, in which only a tonal center—either a note or a chord of any kind—is implied, with the relationships of all the other notes and chords left undefined. This use of "tonality" when applicable merely means that at some point of the work of music some of the notes momentarily take on a semblance of stability. As an organizing principle, it will not carry us very far, although when some critics insist that Schoenberg's music of the period 1908–1913 is tonal, all they mean is that these points of stability exist.

sway, and acts as a means of creating tension. Since dissonance is the essential expressive element of music, and modulation is dissonance on the large scale, it makes expression *for the first time an element of the total structure.* The concept of modulation was eventually to prove the powerful force that corrupted tonality.

By the beginning of the eighteenth century the tonal piece had become a work in which the tonic triad (or the key) acted as a frame and in which another triad—generally the dominant triad, but other, more remote relationships were introduced—acted as a secondary polar force within the music, momentarily appearing as itself a tonic or a new key. In order for this to take place, there had to be a chord or set of chords that acted as a pivot between the original key and the new one; that is, there had to be at least one moment when the listener could not be certain what the key really was. This was the crucial moment of modulation and always carried a latent possibility of dramatic and expressive effect. It was the inspiration of the later eighteenth century and even more of the nineteenth to extend and expand this moment of ambiguity.

From a chord that could be interpreted as being in either of two keys, composers came to long phrases and passages that created the same ambiguity. There are many ways to do this: one is to pass so rapidly through a series of keys that none of them achieves stability. This was already a common practice by the time of Bach. Another is the use of a succession of chords such that either their order or their dissonance makes the passage as a whole impossible to interpret in any given tonality. With Chopin and Liszt, this was not only one of the fundamental methods for creating dramatic tension but was even used in a purely ornamental fashion. The chromaticism of the style greatly increased: the power of the simple dominant as the basic polar force against the tonic gradually weakened during the early nineteenth century, and much more remote triads were used instead.

The subdominant triad and those related to it were now often polarized, or turned into secondary tonics. Since the subdominant was essentially an "antidominant," and the tonic is itself the dominant of the subdominant, this development increasingly and inevitably weakened the central role of the tonic. In early Romantic music, indeed, the tonic had already lost some of the power it held in eighteenth-century style.

When we come to Wagner, the expansion of the crucial moment of ambiguity attained monumental proportions. There are many pages where no single phrase can be interpreted as belonging to a fixed key, and where certain chords have more than two possible interpretations. To achieve this fluidity the chromaticism has become all-pervasive. This suspension of clear small-scale harmonic sense is what enabled Wagner to give the impression of long-range action, in which the music proceeds in a series of waves and not in small articulated steps. Simple tonal explanations of certain sections of the later works of Wagner often break down even when valid tonal analyses of the smaller elements within them can be given. The polarizing function of modulation has been developed so far and so radically that the resistance of the framework that gives it its meaning—the tonic triad—has been weakened beyond repair. The dramatic power of tonality has begun to destroy it from within.

Tonality is more than a harmonic system (although it is sometimes convenient to speak as if it were only that).

It carries with it a complex set of presuppositions about melody, rhythm, and form, none of which can exist independently of the others. Most of our ideas of musical form are still today derived from tonality: the tonic triad's function as a frame within which each note takes on a decisive meaning implies a symmetrical form to which all the elements of music responded. The *da capo,* ternary, or simple ABA form is the simplest of the ways this symmetry could manifest itself: a more sophisticated type is "sonata-form," in which the symmetry requires that music which appears first as a move away from the tonic toward a newly polarized key be reinterpreted finally within the tonic area in order to restore the balance. We can see the strains that the language of tonality was undergoing by the third decade of the nineteenth century when both the *da capo* and "sonata" forms began to seem old-fashioned, badly equipped to fulfill the demands of contemporary musical thought. Much more fluid, less symmetrical shapes were now indispensable.

These strains, too, were revealed in a more subtle and more troubling manner by the loss of efficiency of the musical language. The new ability, through chromaticism and dissonance, to suspend the clear sense of key in certain passages or even for pages was eroding the lucid hierarchical structure of the triads. Within tonality, expression depends first upon the individual dissonance and then, on a higher level, upon the relation of each chord and each section of the work to the tonic center. The intelligibility of this relation was largely disappearing throughout the nineteenth century. The clarity of the simpler relations was being sacrificed to the physical effect, the sense of excitement that could be stimulated by the more remote modulations.[6] With the music of Max Reger, the most remote key relationships became equivalent in weight and importance to the simple ones; almost no difference is perceptible.

The same disintegration took place within the phrase as well as in the larger sense of key and form. Exotic combinations of chords were made to play the role of common ones. For this reason, the corresponding symmetrical rhythmic skeleton of the phrase began to buckle, as it was so closely dependent on harmonic tensions. Even the handling of tone color and orchestration was influenced: when the precise harmonic function of each note was no longer clearly perceptible, orchestral effects had to be laid on more lavishly and with a much heavier hand. In the tone poems of Richard Strauss, for example, there is a considerable amount of busy-work in which the details were never intended to be distinguished and which is composed in such a way that it could not be clearly and distinctly played. (Strauss is known to have been disconcerted by the growing virtuosity of modern orchestras and their ability to give an unfortunate clarity to passages written to sound as a sweeping and harmonious blur.)

By the end of the century, the final appearance of the tonic chord in many works of Strauss, Reger, and others sounded like a polite bow in the direction of academic theory; the rest of the music has often proceeded as if it made no difference with what triad it ended. The music

[6]The further away from the tonic that we go along the circle of fifths, the less precisely can the significance of the relation to the tonic be defined. When the modulation is a dramatic and surprising one, we often cannot tell if the new key is being approached from the dominant or subdominant direction, on which much of the significance depends.

is, much of the time, in some key or other, but there is no longer any sense of direction. It is rarely evident whether the music is moving away from, or settling in, any given tonality, and even clear sections of stable tonality sometimes have no specific relation to a total scheme. The degree of stability has become only a localized effect, never a generalized one.

Schoenberg's sense of the irrelevance of this occasional and superficial return to the formal clarity of tonal harmony was decisive for the step he took in 1909. As he himself wrote about his String Quartet no. 2 in F-sharp minor of 1908:

> In the third and fourth movements the key is presented distinctly at all the main dividing points of the formal organization. Yet the overwhelming multitude of dissonances cannot be balanced any longer by occasional returns to such tonal triads as represent a key. It seemed inadequate to force a movement into the Procrustean bed of a tonality without supporting it by harmonic progressions that pertain to it. This was my concern, and it should have occupied the mind of all my contemporaries also.[7]

It did, of course, occupy other minds than Schoenberg's: Debussy declared that one must get rid of tonality, and Skryabin went a considerable distance in dissolving tonal relations into complete chromaticism. Stravinsky and Ives, at this time, often treated tonal relations with a sort of ironic distancing effect, like quotations from a language already so archaic as to be slightly foreign.

If no one was so thorough as Schoenberg in his renunciation of tonality, it is paradoxically because no one was so deeply attached as he to certain aspects of it. The

[7]Cited in Willi Reich, *Schoenberg,* p. 31.

contradictions increasingly evident in the loose employment of tonal relations as a central background for un-
controlled chromatic experiment had become intolerable to him. For him, either tonality meant a method of
tonal integration, total control over every element of the
work—or it meant nothing. In the 1920s and later, he
made bitter fun of composers who wrote "pseudo-tonal"
music—that is, music which paid occasional lip service
to the stability of the central triad without acknowledg-
ing the whole system of relations that this stability logi-
cally entailed.

When Alban Berg, in a passionate apology for atonal
music given many years later in an interview, said in
opening the defense, "The main thing to show—one may
as well begin with the crucial point—is that the melody,
the principal part, the theme, is the basis, or determines
the course of this, as of all other, music," he put his finger
—unwittingly, it seems—on one of the principal symp-
toms of the collapse of tonality. It is certainly true that
melody was the principal basis of form in all nineteenth-
century music after the death of Beethoven, but that was
because harmonic relationships no longer possessed the
force and influence they had throughout the eighteenth
century. The present tendency of musicology to make
harmony almost the sole determinant of late-eighteenth-
century form, with melody and rhythm reduced to mere
attendants, is unwarranted, but it is a corrective to a
radical misunderstanding. Form in the nineteenth century is determined by the repetition, variation, and development of themes; in the eighteenth it was an inter-
play between harmonic movement, thematic identity,
and phrase structure. How far harmony had lost its
power by the end of the nineteenth may be seen by the
explanation, in part misleading, that Schoenberg him-

self gave for the new concentration of dissonance in early-twentieth-century works, which he ascribed to the new-found independence of contrapuntal writing: "the individual parts proceed regardless of whether or not their meeting results in codified harmonies."

But the source of the dissonance of early Schoenberg (or of Skryabin, Strauss, and Debussy) is not merely harmonic (or vertical) but melodic (or horizontal): that is, the melodies no longer imply pure tonal relations, and played by themselves alone they would defy attempts to interpret them coherently within a system of triads. Schoenberg's attempt, in discussing his atonal music, to put tonal harmony to an atonal theme only makes it sound insipid. It is not, as Schoenberg thought, that the contrapuntal independence makes harmonic interpretation difficult, but rather that the individual melodies themselves (which Schoenberg, like so many nineteenth-century composers, considered the basis of inspiration, that aspect of the work that was *given* to the composer) are no longer conceived in terms of triads and therefore demand a free-moving polyphonic texture.

The melodies of early Schoenberg—like those of any composer from 1700 to 1900—gain their expressive intensity largely through the dissonance implied by the curves they outline, by the juxtaposition of notes which, played together, form dissonant intervals, and by the emphasis of these dissonances by wide skips within the melodic curves. From Bach to Brahms these dissonances are always conceived as implying a context of triads *within the melody itself.* Already in the music of Brahms, this triadic chordal progression is beginning to weaken: the dissonance is that of a dissonant interval rather than that of dissonance to a triad. The triads can still be added by the accompaniment without strain, and there is a peculiar poignancy in Brahms's music that comes from the disparity of the acute dissonances traced by the melody and the rich, mellifluous harmony that supports and surrounds them. The expressiveness of Schoenberg's melodies goes naked, and an attempt to resolve them by harmony would only travesty them.

The breakdown of the harmonic and tonal conception of large form has, therefore, its analogue in the character of the melodies. Western music, at least since 1500, has been organized in terms of a symmetrical correspondence and even a reciprocal influence between the largest aspects of form and the smallest detail. A lack of correspondence is either a sign of the composer's incompetence, or else a source of expression—a structural dissonance, in short, that can be confirmed only by being resolved elsewhere in the work, by restoring the correspondence. In the eighteenth century a musical phrase contained within itself the movement away from the tonic that was the basis of the large structure. Schoenberg's contemptuous phrase "pseudo-tonal composers" was meant to indicate those of his contemporaries for whom the lack of correspondence between detail and large form was a matter of no concern, and who accepted the growing contradictions of the musical language not even as something to exploit but as an unpleasant condition of life which it would be best to ignore, as one averts one's eyes from poverty and vice. More than any other composer, Schoenberg faced what he felt was the misery of contemporary music.

In comparison with the latitudinarian who believed that all forms of expression, no matter how debased, have a right to life, the man who hated all contemporary music was an honorable antagonist. In many respects, Schoenberg was at one with him. "That is the kind of music I should really like to write," he once said, smiling, to Roberto Gerhard after a performance of the Grieg piano concerto. And when Webern proposed programing Schoenberg's Music for a Film Sequence for a concert in Barcelona, where Schoenberg had been living for almost a year, he protested half-seriously, "I have made many friends here who have never heard my works but who play tennis with me. What will they think of me when they hear my horrible dissonances?" The music-lover who was terrified by the new dissonance and by the loss of the old habits of musical understanding had Schoenberg's ironical sympathy. He reserved his denunciation for the musician who acquiesced willingly in the incoherence of contemporary music, who accepted the new dissonance and the new chromaticism provided that occasional triads were introduced from time to time, however unconvincingly, as lightning-conductors. Pseudo-tonal music seemed essentially hypocritical, an indulgence in all the voluptuous chromatic sins while giving them a whitewash of tonal virtue.

We no longer need to take so strong a moral position: music that accepts an outward pretense of tonality while aspiring to a freedom in the use of dissonance which annuls the possibility of a rigorous and intense use of tonal relations is still being written today. It is even capable of sustaining a personal style (that of Paul Hindemith or Benjamin Britten, for example), although it necessitates retreating from the ideal of original invention that has been imposed on art since the Renaissance. Originality requires the exploration of a self-created universe coherent and rich enough to offer possibilities beyond the development of an individual manner. An individual style built upon the placid acquiescence in a disintegrating language is stamped, too, with a peculiar character; it is reduced to the exploiting of a limited set of mannerisms (*ostinato,* or repeating basses, in the case of Britten). Schoenberg's achievement was not only or even primarily a personal one, and out of his vision came a Second Viennese School, the work of Webern, Berg, and himself along with many minor figures, and an influence that has surpassed that of Bartók and even perhaps of Stravinsky.

Schoenberg's own personal voice, however, is already evident in works written as early as *Verklaerte Nacht* and the *Gurrelieder*—an acutely expressive one with a love for asymmetrical phrase and a flowing contrapuntal intricacy. The tone poem *Pelleas und Melisande,* written in 1902–1903, is less characteristically personal, but it is remarkable for its attempt to combine a classicistic "sonata-form" with a scenario derived from a play and for the immense size of the orchestral forces required. In the Chamber Symphony no. 1, opus 9, completed in 1906, there is again an attempt, which derives clearly from the Liszt sonata, to make a single sonata-form integrate entire works in several movements played without a break between them, and a similar essay is found in the Quartet no. 1 of 1905. The harmonic complexity in these works strains both the tonal structure and the thematic form to the limit. The strain is even greater in the Quartet no. 2 of 1908. All these works are still Brahmsian in phrase structure, and their coherence is attained above all by the continuously varying employment of the same motifs. Form is still a thematic conception for Schoenberg; we follow the piece almost entirely by recognizing the motifs and their transformations.

The really revolutionary act was less the destruction of the tonal frame with the *George-Lieder* of 1909 than the renunciation of thematic form as well with *Erwartung* in the same year. In this work Schoenberg did away with all the traditional means in which music was supposed to make itself intelligible: repetition of themes, integrity and discursive transformation of clearly recognizable motifs,[8] harmonic structure based on a framework of tonality. There is no fully developed sense of key anywhere in *Erwartung,* and each motif that appears is abandoned after a few seconds. Nevertheless, *Erwartung* is one of the most effective, easily accessible, and immediately convincing of Schoenberg's works. This apparently total freedom from the requirements of musical form has made *Erwartung* a well-attested miracle, inexplicable and incontrovertible.

Concert performances of *Erwartung* have become relatively frequent, although stage productions are very rare. A monodrama for soprano and orchestra, the opera requires numerous rapid and expensive changes of scene: in addition, the work lasts only about twenty-five minutes, so that it is even less attractive to operatic im-

[8]In a recent work by Jan Maegaard, *Studien zur Entwicklung des dodekaphonen Satzes bei Arnold Schönberg* (Copenhagen, 1972), there is a masterly and lengthy discussion of the strong family resemblances between the motifs in one subsection and those in others, and of the consequent unity of melodic and harmonic material. Maegaard concludes, however, that no melodic contour in this work is sufficiently characterized so that it can function as a theme: "No melodic form can be called more basic or 'thematic' than any other" (page 318), and he adds that to analyze the development of one type of motif throughout the work would be an analysis without a point of reference or with only arbitrary points of reference, as the various types are subjected to continuous variation and blend one into the other. For Maegaard, this athematic structure of *Erwartung* (in spite of traces of thematic function) arises from the absolute equivalence and interchange of harmony and melody (or of the horizontal and vertical axes of music) in this work.

presarios, who know that double bills are not generally a success (except, of course, for the traditional *Cavalleria Rusticana* and *Pagliacci*, and their popularity seems to be dying). The libretto was written by Marie Pappenheim, largely, it seems, under Schoenberg's direction and according to his requirements. It is unclear how much of the action is realistic, how much purely symbolic in this nightmare vision of a woman who imagines that her lover is dead—or, indeed, has she herself killed him? In subject and atmosphere, it is the quintessential expressionist work.

Erwartung is traditionally supposed to be the despair of musical analysis; the description I have given above is negative: athematic, atonal. Not everyone is in complete agreement with this description and one writer[9] has even recognized the fleeting appearance of a melody in *Erwartung*, a quotation from an early song in D minor by Schoenberg himself: it may be found just before the end of the 401st of 426 measures, and even there it is hidden in the cellos, followed a few seconds later by a repetition and an inversion in the bass clarinet and bassoons. Other writers, George Perle in particular, have found an occasional foreshadowing of the later twelve-tone technique, in which the harmony may arise out of the successive transformations of a complex chord. Still others, such as Robert Craft, dismiss the terms "athematic" and "atonal" and hear a constant motivic development—but his principal motif (the only example, in fact, that he gives) is A–B-flat–A—three notes with only two pitches. Stückenschmidt hears the recurrence of D–F–C-sharp. This would be enough motivic structure

[9] Herbert H. Buchanan, "A Key to Schoenberg's *Erwartung*, op. 17," *Journal of the American Musicological Society*, xx, 3, 1967.

for Beethoven or for Brahms to construct a large work, and these figures, along with many others, are indeed pervasive in *Erwartung*. But in music before Schoenberg, each separate occurrence of a motif connects with the others either as part of a larger continuity or by being placed in a context that clearly recalls—through a similarity of harmony or texture—its other appearances; it is by this continuity and these similarities that we are able to maintain the identity of the motif. But this continuity and similarity are both refused us by Schoenberg. Every eighteenth-century work, for example, is full of rising and descending thirds, but nothing permits us to claim this as a motif until it is *contextually* given this status within the work, and for this there must be a confluence of rhythm, harmony, and texture lacking in *Erwartung*.

If Schoenberg's achievement is not to be minimized, then some coherence must be given to the analytic terms "motif" and "tonal": only then can we deal with the important aspects of the phenomena convincingly pointed out by Craft and, above all, Perle. *Erwartung* is "atonal" in the sense that the tonal functions of tonic and dominant no longer exist; there are, in fact, almost no perfect triads in this work that could even suggest these functions. It is "tonal" only in a weak sense: certain chords are used to create momentary centers of stability, and these chords vary throughout. *Erwartung* is "athematic" or "nonmotivic" in the sense that understanding and appreciating it does not require recognizing the motifs from one part of the work to another as all music from Bach to Stravinsky demands: about thirty seconds is the limit of time required of the listener in *Erwartung* within which a recognition of a shape may be expected; outside this limit the recurrences of a certain set of pitches are not fortuitous, but they do not define a simple entity whose transformation throughout the work determines its meaning. Craft himself (in the program notes to his recording) admits that "the web of motives in *Erwartung* is extremely difficult to disentangle," and ascribes this to "the unprecedented complexity of musical texture." This seems to me a halfway step to the truth: the "web of motives" is not concealed by the texture but a product of the texture itself.

What Schoenberg, consciously or unconsciously, realized before anyone else is that the concept of themes and the system of motivic construction were bound up with a symmetrical system of harmony clearly oriented around a central triad. What gives the "motif" its significance and its solidity in a work written between 1700 and 1900 is its movement within a symmetrical and stable structure defined by modulation away from, and back to, a perfect triad. Schoenberg was not the first composer to abandon "triadic" harmony; but he was the first to realize fully the implications of such a revolution for all the other aspects of musical form. It might even be said that no one else in this century has taken tonality as seriously as Schoenberg, and the years of *Erwartung* and *Pierrot Lunaire* were also taken up by the writing of a gigantic and conservative textbook on tonal harmony.

But we need not, with George Perle, throw up our hands at *Erwartung* and speak of its "amorphous continuity . . . a kind of stream of consciousness writing that defies objective analysis"; it is a paradoxical stand for Perle to take as he himself has made some excellent observations on the harmony of the opening pages of *Erwartung,* with the reappearance and transformation of chords that give an obvious unity and stability to the sound. Unfortunately Perle's model for this process is a chord with four notes, and Schoenberg's procedure is both more and less complex.

Almost all of the chords in *Erwartung* have six notes, and this texture is fairly consistent throughout the work. But this six-note chord is generally made up of two three-note chords outlining the seventh, e.g., a fourth above an augmented fourth:

Two of these chords put together make a very handsome sound:

and (along with these chords) we find the following *in the first two measures alone,* either as simple combinations or outlined by the melody:

All these chords contain a major seventh (except for the last two which are inversions of such chords). There is no proper term in tonal harmony for such chords, and I shall call them "seventh chords" from here on (and hope that there will be no confusion with the traditional seventh chords of tonality). These "major seventh chords" may be combined with augmented triads:

(which gives the harmony outlined by voice, oboe, and cellos in measure 6), and with "minor seventh chords." These give innumerable permutations, but all have a unified and easily recognizable chromatic sonority, and we may say that they fill the musical space of *Erwartung.*[10]

These six-note chords give an extraordinary consistency to the harmonic texture of *Erwartung,* and they were to play the fundamental role in the development of Schoenberg's style for the rest of his life. They have obviously replaced the triad as the basic element of composition: their presence throughout the score gives them the kind of stabilizing force previously possible only to the perfect triad.

Here we touch on the most delicate and most difficult to understand of all Schoenberg's innovations: his reconstruction of the relation of consonance and dissonance without the use of the perfect triad, which had been the ground of this relation for more than four centuries. The "seventh chord" is no longer a dissonance for Schoenberg but a point of rest; it never, however, reaches absolute stability, for which Schoenberg was to create a totally new basis.

For the moment, we must concentrate on his reconstruction of relative degrees of stability, that subtly nuanced wavering between intense anguish and half-resolution which is so characteristic of *Erwartung.* The simplest and most localized device for achieving this is described by Schoenberg himself at the end of the *Harmonielehre,* but with a certain hesitation as if he did

[10]What is rare in *Erwartung* is the perfect triad, except when in a combined major-minor form: making the inversion of a "seventh chord."

not himself quite understand the technique he had
created. It concerns an implied resolution that does not
in fact take place. In a discussion of the attenuation of
the harshness of dissonances by spacing the dissonant
notes far apart, Schoenberg gives a chord from *Erwartung* of thirteen notes, which embraces eleven different
notes of the chromatic scale plus two octave doublings.
He observes that a resolution of the two upper notes
into consonances according to the rules of tonal harmony appears to be implied by the structure of the
chord, and that this allusion to older forms seems to
have a satisfying effect even though the resolution does
not actually occur.[11] Schoenberg himself realized the
important role that the older style was to play in his
work.

It is not, however, on a strictly harmonic basis that the
rules of classical "tonal" harmony are implied in
Schoenberg's music after 1908. Effects of dissonance and
resolution arise here largely from the melodic lines and
the phrasing implied by the rhythm—although, if we
remember that notes of a single melodic line can be conceived as dissonant or consonant to each other, we will
admit that an exact separation of melody and harmony
is not possible.

In fact, to the end of his life, Schoenberg wrote music
whose rhythm and phrasing recalled the late Romantic
style with which he had started. The rise and fall of his
melodies imply the tonal oscillation from agitation to
stability, and, although the strict sense of cadence, with

[11]What Schoenberg appears not to remark is that it is just
these two upper notes, E-flat and C, that are doubled (two and
three octaves below respectively), and that this gives them a
stability denied to the other notes of the chord. See *Harmonielehre*, pp. 499–500.

its final absolute consonance, is not possible for Schoenberg, the feeling of cadence is re-created by the linear shape of each contrapuntal voice in his music. Here is revealed one part of the secret of the continuous and violent expressivity of Schoenberg's music: the expressive force, finding no outlet in a large "homophonic" harmonic structure, pervades the melodic line of all the different instruments and voices. In Schoenberg, there is no voice, no note that is expressively neutral.

This radical expressivity, congenial to Schoenberg's temperament, and obviously closely related to the movements in the other arts of his time, is therefore also a logical development of his extension of the musical language. Technically speaking, it may be described as a displacement of the harmonic tension to the melodic line.

The displacement also includes what may be called the musical texture. Schoenberg has already given us a hint of this by his observation of the relation of dissonance to the spacing—a relation very much part of the musical consciousness of the time: perhaps the greatest master of the spacing of dissonant chords is Debussy. But such spacings are only a small part of musical texture, and it is in the almost unbelievable variety and significance of its textures that *Erwartung* is most revolutionary. It is here above all that the fundamental effects of dissonance and resolution are reconstructed. Dissonance, banished from harmony, had returned transformed to take over all the other elements of music.

The most remarkable innovations in texture concern three aspects of this elusive subject: rhythm, orchestral color, and harmonic spacing or concentration. It is in the field of rhythm that the large form of *Erwartung* is most immediately perceptible. Two kinds of rhythmic texture

alternate throughout the work: sections with continuously repeating figures *(ostinati)* are followed by others
of either stable or continuously changing material. This
contrast between passages with a marked *ostinato* effect
and those with no repeating figures of any kind is the
chief instrument in the definition of the dramatic action
of the monodrama.

An *ostinato* figure is ambiguous in its sense of movement: it is neither stable nor dynamic.[12] An *ostinato* creates small-scale motion, but since it remains unchanged,
it prevents any large harmonic movement. Nevertheless,
an *ostinato* creates instability and contributes to the
larger rhythm through the tension that comes from insistent repetition: this gives a clear method for recon-
structing the effect of dissonance (as Beethoven already
knew, when he turned a consonance into a dissonance
merely by incorporating it into an *ostinato*). An *ostinato*
that both accelerates and increases in volume can create
an almost unbearable tension.

By their contrast with the *ostinato,* the sections with
no repeating figures can give an impression either of
moving with great speed—a burst of energy after the
repressed force of the *ostinato* section—or else of almost
complete calm, a sense of clear resolution after the tension of the *ostinato.* It is above all in these latter sections
of relative stability that Schoenberg was able to employ
that extraordinary new technique of orchestration that
he had developed only a few months previous to *Erwartung* with the Five Pieces for Orchestra.

In this work, Schoenberg's debt to Mahler is immedi-

[12]Rhythm must include the rate of change of harmony, as well
as the actual note-values. If the same harmony is repeated, then
the harmonic rhythm is zero, while the note values may be very
fast and have complex time-values.

ately apparent; like Mahler he calls only at moments for the entire force of the very large orchestra necessary for the work and generally uses small groups of solo instruments. This makes a kind of chamber-music sound in which the combinations of instruments are continually shifting. (This technique is carried even further in *Erwartung,* where sixteen first violins and fourteen seconds are called for but used all at once only at a very few points.) Each phrase can be given an entirely new instrumental color, and is consequently characterized less by its harmonic content than by the instrumental combination that embodies it.

This emancipation of tone color was as significant and as characteristic of the first decades of the twentieth century as the emancipation of dissonance. Tone color was released from its complete subordination to pitch in musical structure: until this point *what* note was played had been far more important than the instrumental color or the dynamics with which it was played. The principal element of music was conceived to be pitch. (This was at least the theoretical position, even if, in practice, other elements were to have had in reality greater weight at rare moments.)

The third of Schoenberg's Five Pieces for Orchestra, called "Chord Colors," was later retitled more fancifully "Summer Morning by a Lake." It begins with a single soft chord triple *pianissimo* that changes instrumental color as its notes are transferred from one instrument to another, with the exits and entrances overlapping. The changes are directed to be played with great subtlety: we should not, in fact, be aware of the individual instruments as they enter but only of the gradual changes of sonority. The orchestration of the first chord changes imperceptibly from a grouping of flutes (low register), clarinets, bassoon, and viola solo to an entirely new color of English horn, bassoon, horns, trumpets (low register), and double-bass solo in a high register. The harmony changes, also slowly and imperceptibly, as the piece proceeds, and new, short motifs play themselves out against this slow-moving background.

This last technique is applied on an even larger scale in *Erwartung,* which not only employs a fantastic range of instrumental color (with all the varieties of fluttertongue, bowing on the bridge of the violins, playing with the wood of the bow, string harmonics, *glissando,* etcetera) but also makes a striking use of an imperceptibly shifting or even completely stable background against which move angular motifs and an intensely lyric recitative may stand out in relief. Here the orchestral color is used to re-create once again a displacement of the dissonance-consonance relation, as the faster-moving motifs dissolve into the background or are resolved into the more stable form of an *ostinato.*

This new eminence of color, texture, and dynamics entails, as a consequence, something that most respectable musicians have been reluctant to admit because it is conceived as something disreputable: the downgrading of the importance of pitch. It is clear that wrong notes matter less in Schoenberg and in many of his contemporaries such as Richard Strauss than they do in Mozart or Wagner: they are even in fact less noticeable. This does not mean that the music of Schoenberg does not sound a good deal better when it is played with the right notes and proper intonation, just as Mozart sounds best when played with the proper dynamics and a great sensitivity to tone color.

From time to time there appear malicious stories of eminent conductors who have not realized that, in a piece of Webern or Schoenberg, the clarinetist, for example, picked up an A instead of a B-flat clarinet and played his part a semitone off. These recurrent tales, often true, do not have the significance given them by those critics who believe that music should have stopped before Debussy, as each individual line in Schoenberg's music and even in Webern's later pointillist style defines a harmonic sense that, *even when transposed,* can fit into the general harmony of the work as a whole. (Here we must remember that harmony is conveyed as powerfully along a musical line as it is by a simultaneous chord.) The attenuation of the traditional concept of dissonance gives a considerable freedom to the movement of the individual instrumental voices, and for this to take place the central position in the hierarchy of musical elements can no longer be given to pitch. What is clear, indeed, is that the simple linear hierarchy must give way to a new and more complex set of relationships in which pitch is only one element among others, and not by any means always the most important.

This explains the absurdity of so many performances of "avant-garde" music, in which the players, proud of having played so many of the right notes, feel they can neglect with a clear conscience the composer's directions for dynamics and phrasing. "My music is not modern," Schoenberg once said; "it is only badly played." In the third piece of *Pierrot Lunaire,* for example, the clarinet part could be transposed a half-step up or down while the other instruments remain at the correct pitch, and (although some effect would be lost) the music would still make sense; but if the dynamics are not respected, the music becomes totally absurd and makes no sense at all. The harmonic content of the piece is conveyed less through the simultaneous chords of the instruments playing together than by the individual lines described by each instrument. That occurs, as I have already emphasized, because the relationship of dissonance has been partially displaced from the interval or the chord on to other aspects of music.

It is in this context that Schoenberg's most controversial invention must be understood: the use in *Pierrot Lunaire* of *Sprechstimme,* or half-speaking, half-singing. This work for quintet and voice (a setting of macabre *fin-de-siècle* poems by a justly forgotten poet, Albert Giraud) is perhaps Schoenberg's most famous work. Schoenberg said that he intended the voice of the singer/ speaker only to touch on the original note and then quickly to leave it, generally by a kind of *glissando* moving to the next note. If the singer/speaker does not actually reach the exact note indicated in the score, this does not have by any means a disastrous effect on the music: a certain improvised freedom of pitch in the vocal part is indeed necessary for a performance of this work. The idea of *Sprechstimme* in *Pierrot Lunaire* carries the destruction of the unique, omnipotent status of pitch in music further than Schoenberg was ever to dare in any other work (although he used *Sprechstimme* again), but he was able to do so because the harmonic consistency is concentrated within the individual lines and cuts across the older concepts of chordal harmony.

This new ideal of harmonic consistency is supported by Schoenberg's idiosyncratic form of motivic construction in parts of *Pierrot Lunaire,* as well as in most of the Five Pieces for Orchestra. A short motif of from three to fourteen notes provides the nucleus not only for the entire melodic development but for almost every note of the accompaniment as well. The eighth piece of *Pierrot Lunaire,* "Night," for example, develops entirely from a ten-note motif: everything can be traced back easily to that kernel. The harmony implied by these motifs pervades the music completely: they are meant to give any work composed by this method an individual and characteristic sonority.

The method is an old one, going back to Bach and even to the late-fifteenth-century Netherlandish composers, and it received the greatest expansion of its range before Schoenberg in the late music of Beethoven and in a new and striking form in Brahms, from whom Schoenberg derives most of his technique of motivic construction. But in music before Schoenberg, the technique governed not the total form (which is based on the concept of tonality) but the creation of detail; only Beethoven was able to relate the development of the smallest details directly to the larger elements, and this by deriving the motivic kernel immediately from the most basic elements of tonality, by which large forms were organized. These tonal principles no longer governed Schoenberg's musical language: the construction of large forms was therefore an overriding problem.

Along with the violence of expression and unparalleled variety of texture and sonority of the music written by Schoenberg and his students Webern and Berg from 1908 to 1913, there comes a development of miniature forms—miniatures, in fact, shorter and more concentrated than any others in the history of music. There is some question whether, in fact, it was Webern or Schoenberg who was first in the creation of these tiny forms. Schoenberg's Six Little Pieces for Piano, opus 19, which are his most remarkable essays in the absolute miniature, were mostly written on February 19, 1911; Webern had already reached extreme brevity by 1910 with the Five Pieces for String Quintet, opus 5, and the Six

Pieces for Orchestra, opus 6. Nevertheless, after Schoenberg's death a manuscript came to light of three little
pieces for chamber orchestra (the third unfinished)
dated February 8, 1910. Once again we must postulate a
community of style and an evident exchange of ideas:
questions of precedence have not much interest when
experiments are carried out so near each other—above
all, when the results seem at least in retrospect to have
been so inevitable a development of the musical situation.

These miniatures are sometimes astonishingly brief,
less than a half-minute or so, and very often extremely
soft throughout as well. The second of Webern's Three
Pieces for Cello and Piano, opus 11, written in 1914, lasts
only thirteen seconds, but two of the Six Pieces for Orchestra, opus 6, of 1909, although each lasts almost a
minute, are even more striking, as they are scored for an
enormous orchestra with quadruple and sextuple wind
and a huge percussion section. The spectacle of enormous forces massed for the purpose of performing such
tiny pieces is evidently as much a provocation as the
stylistic violence of other contemporary manifestations.
The miniature form is, of course, peculiarly apt in its
compression for conveying the expressive intensity so
important in this period. These miniatures of Webern,
Berg, and Schoenberg do not diminish the emotions
they express but enlarge them, as if fragments of feeling
were blown up by a powerful microscope. They give,
indeed, less the impression of fragments than of complete
works, but only because the great variety of color and
sound they contain implies a fierce, laconic repression
that forces a large gesture into a rigid and cramped
space.

The miniatures of Webern are among the most striking and accessible achievements of this period: to them must be added the exquisite early *Altenberg* (or *Post-Card*) *Songs* of Berg. Even if opus 19 of Schoenberg post-dates the earliest true miniatures by a few months, the technique that went into these miniatures is largely of Schoenberg's devising. This technique is that of motivic construction, in which a small kernel provides the complete material for the work. What made the miniatures possible was Schoenberg's relentless and almost fanatical concentration on motif already evident in the early works of 1909: the song cycle *Book of the Hanging Garden* on poems by Stefan George. (The first real miniatures of Webern are, indeed, his settings of poems of George, which are exactly contemporary with Schoenberg's cycle.)

The problem of the large forms remained, and it was, in fact, to both Schoenberg and Webern the crucial and —at least so it seemed—the insoluble problem. The recognition of form, they understood, demanded the recognition of similarities, of invariances: for form to exist, something had to be repeated, had to retain its identity throughout its transformations. Yet the disappearance of tonal harmony had made the large-scale symmetries on which the recognition of form seemed to depend an empty gesture. The return of a theme in the tonic key in a nineteenth-century sonata was an inner necessity: a similar return in an atonal work was arbitrary.

There was, above all in *Pierrot Lunaire,* an attempt to solve the problem on a scale intermediate between small and large by contrapuntal devices, principally that of canon.[13] We may say that the canon is essentially for

[13]The canon is a form in which every voice sings the same line but enters at a different moment (as in "Row, row, row your boat, gently down the stream"). In complicated forms the origi-

Schoenberg a large extension of motivic construction, containing the same principle of one set of notes, now a much longer set, providing the basis for the whole work. "The Moonspot," number 18 of *Pierrot Lunaire,* is one of the most elaborate canons worked out since the end of the fifteenth century; like other works based on a nuclear motif, however, it is entirely dominated by the shape of the opening melody, which reappears throughout in different forms. There are many other examples of such contrapuntal construction, including an early song by Webern on a poem by Richard Dehmel, "Helle Nacht," published posthumously, and written in triple invertible counterpoint (in which any one of three voices may be played both above and below the two others).

The use of such contrapuntal devices as canon and invertible counterpoint provides the traditional occasions for demonstrating a composer's virtuosity. While the ingenuity of design of Schoenberg's canons may dazzle and charm, the virtuosity, however, has vanished with the disappearance of tonal harmony. The difficulty of the tonal canon consisted almost entirely in the proper resolution of dissonance and most of all in the correct placing of the final absolute consonance, the tonic chord. The atonal canon presents no great harmonic difficulties —which is not to underrate the free imagination that may go into its elaboration.

As long as no substitute had been found for the absolute final consonance of tonal music, the creation of large forms would remain a problem: absolute consonance is a final demarcation of form. With it, the limits of the form are indicated: and they can be approached at

_____

nal line may be introduced backward, upside-down, twice as fast or slow, etcetera.

the pace determined by the composer. No composer of the early twentieth century was willing to settle for musical forms whose outlines were vague or indeterminate, left to chance or to some force outside control. From Aristotle on, an artistic form was above all *defined*, its limits clearly discernible.

The limits of small forms could be determined in various ways, the technique of the nuclear motif being the simplest: when the various permutations and combinations of the motif had been sufficiently displayed, when they had made a musical or expressive point, the piece was over. If the motif was only two to five notes long, some such feeling of satiety was not hard to attain. In addition, the coherence of style of these miniatures was safeguarded in ways already mentioned: a consistency of harmony based on chords of similar construction (often related to a motif), and a sense of *relative* degrees of dissonance through a parody technique of the older tonal style in phrasing and rhythm and through an elaborate and highly sophisticated sense of texture and color.

Only with *Erwartung*, however, did the Schoenberg of 1908–1913 solve the problem of a unified large-scale work. In one sense, of course, *Erwartung* may be described as a series of miniatures, each little section characterized by its own motif and an idiosyncratic texture, even by its own orchestra as the groups of instruments change from section to section but remain to some extent stable within them. (In the same way, Schoenberg, using only five players, manages to achieve a different instrumentation for each song in *Pierrot Lunaire.*) The form of each section itself is based—like most of the miniatures of this period—on nuclear motivic development, on the elaboration of a tiny motif or even of two or three motifs which determine the melody and the harmonic complex as well. The motifs of different sections resemble each other (although without being given sufficient individuality to make an effect of formal repetition, which Schoenberg specifically and conscientiously avoided in this work): the resemblance is based on their relation to the seventh chords that control and unify the work.

This harmonic and motivic consistency, however, is a unifying principle of a passive and negative sort; it cannot determine the shape of a work, and *Erwartung* has a shape, related to the libretto but intelligible independently, as is true of all great operatic music. There is here the sense of movement toward—and away from—absolute consonance, coming in a series of waves. To see Schoenberg's extraordinary substitute for the tonic chord, the absolute consonance of traditional Western music, we must turn to the last measures of the opera.

The last page of *Erwartung* has been so much imitated that it is hard to perceive its originality today, although it still makes an effect that is overpowering. "Oh, are you there," cries the woman about her dead lover, and then adds softly, "I searched," as the low woodwinds begin, triple *pianissimo,* a rising chromatic series of six-note chords. The other instruments enter with similar chords moving up or down the chromatic scale, each group moving at different rates of speed; the fastest speeds come in the last three beats with the dynamics remaining between triple and quadruple *pianissimo.*

This massed chromatic movement at different speeds, both up and down and accelerating, is a saturation of the musical space in a few short seconds; and in a movement that gets ever faster, every note in the range of the orchestra is played in a kind of *glissando.* The saturation of musical space is Schoenberg's substitute for the tonic chord of the traditional musical language. The absolute consonance is a state of chromatic plenitude.

This concept of the saturation of chromatic space as a fixed point toward which the music moves, as a point of rest and resolution, lies behind not just *Erwartung* alone but much of the music of the period. Its importance for the future of music was fundamental. It can take two forms, strong and weak. The weak form is the more common, and became, indeed, canonical by the 1920s, although it was influential long before then: this is the filling out of chromatic space by playing all twelve notes of the chromatic scale in some individual order determined by the composer but without regard to the register, high or low. The strong form, found in *Erwartung* and in a very few other works, fills out the whole of the space in all the registers, or approaches this total saturation.

The weak form acknowledges the primacy of the octave, as most music does. The octave is the first and most powerful overtone, and the acknowledgment is an admission of the power of nature: it is a component of every sound, and we agree that the octave is in some sense the same note as the one below by giving it always the same name. The tyranny of the octave is the tyranny of nature, but it is a tyranny all the same, and there have always been attempts at revolt; the attempts to give displacements of register new musical significance that are found most markedly in Beethoven and Stravinsky are evidence that an acceptance of the facts of nature is a thin basis for the construction of a musical style. *Erwartung* partially escapes from the tyranny of the octave by its pervasive use of "seventh chords," so consistent and omnipresent that they begin to seem as stable as octaves, to take on the functions of consonance. This perhaps makes possible the stroke of genius on its last page, the strong form of total saturation. But the weak form exists on almost every other page: most of the chords in this work, as I have said, contain six notes, and two six-note chords in succession, properly chosen, can cover the twelve notes of the chromatic scale. The large movement of the end toward consonant fullness occurs on a smaller level throughout as each section moves toward the stability of all the notes of the chromatic scale in various combinations, often as simultaneous chords.

This tendency toward the filling out of space[14] was formally although somewhat diffidently acknowledged by both Schoenberg and Webern, as well as by other contemporaries, but the implications were not completely realized. By 1913, a composer named Josef Hauer had developed a technique of composing music that consisted essentially of writing the chromatic scale over and over again in a different order each time. Schoenberg was obliged to treat this silly system with an appearance of respect because of its superficial resemblance to the serialism he was to work out later in the early 1920s. But most composers must have been aware of the tendency to fill out the chromatic space as a kind of gravitational force.

Most revealing is an observation in Schoenberg's *Harmonielehre* on the six-note chords that, as we have seen, form the primary stuff of *Erwartung* and other pieces of Schoenberg at this time. Schoenberg remarks that a first chord of this type is generally followed by a second chord

[14]The metaphor of chromatic "space" is necessary when one wishes to denote the theoretical coexistence of all possible notes that can be played. Our concept of music today is still that of fixed, determinate points called notes. These points are discontinuous: even a *glissando* or slide from one to the other cannot alter this, as only the end points have a true function of pitch.

that contains as many notes as possible that are, in Schoenberg's words, "chromatic heightenings" of the first—that is, that are a minor second above those of the first and that fill out the rest of the chromatic scale. These minor seconds of the superimposed chord are generally *in a different register* from the notes they heighten, and—what is even more important for our argument here—according to Schoenberg, who confesses to not understanding why, *they do not sound like minor seconds*—that is, they do not sound like dissonances, and they imply no need for resolution. In short, in tonality, the piling up of seconds creates tension; in Schoenberg's music after 1908, however, the filling out of the chromatic space is clearly a movement toward stability and resolution. The use of distant registers both brings in the textural play that has now so much greater weight than before, and also serves to imply the total chromatic space whose saturation is the strong form of cadence and resolution.

In heavily chromatic music of the eighteenth and nineteenth centuries this movement toward the filling out of the chromatic scale is already observable: when Mozart or Beethoven wrote in a minor key, they often (particularly in C minor) used a concentration of diminished-seventh chords. Three of these chords (those on F-sharp, G, and A-flat, or any of the inversions of these chords) fill out the chromatic scale completely and without redundancy. When one of these diminished-sevenths occurs, it is most frequently followed closely by the two others. The tendency to fill out the chromatic space becomes naturally more marked by the middle of the nineteenth century: Liszt's music, for example, relies heavily on a continuous succession of the three diminished-seventh chords that map out the scale without

redundancy; the second two-measure phrase of the Prelude to *Tristan und Isolde* of Wagner prominently dis-
plays the four notes of the chromatic scale that are omit-
ted in the first. A missing note was a void, a moment of
tension like a dissonance.

Each work of music defines the space implied by the
musical language that lies at its basis. The filling of the
voids in a chromatic work is evidently as much a natural
instinct as the recognition of the perfect triads of tonality. "When you have written ten notes of the chromatic
scale," a composer once said to me, "the temptation to
add the remaining two is irresistible."

It is clear that within tonality itself—considered not as
an absolute law of nature but as a historical system that
lasted from about 1500 to 1900—there were alternative
and subordinate means of creating the relation of dissonance and consonance, based on rhythm and phrase
structure and dynamics. One of the most important was
the concept of chromaticism, which contains a kind of
magnetic impulse to fill out the space. It may be said,
therefore, that tonality contained within itself the element of its own destruction. The growth of this magnetic
power is evident in the development of music in the
nineteenth century: it was Schoenberg's genius to have
recognized almost unconsciously the dispossession of
the principal means of musical expression by the new
force of what had been a subordinate and contributing
element.

Webern, in 1912, once found himself—without knowing
exactly why he did this—writing down the twelve notes
of the chromatic scale in his notebook and then crossing
off the individual notes as they appeared in one of his
miniature pieces. He was convinced that he had already
written one of the notes of the scale in the work, and that

therefore he need not use it again. The condition for resolution was the filling out of the chromatic scale: a redundancy, a note played twice, was beginning to seem like a dissonance, a disturbance of order. "I had the feeling," Webern wrote, "that when the twelve notes had been played, the piece was over." The miniatures are the natural expression, therefore, of this new form of cadence. The history of the so-called Second Viennese School—Schoenberg, Berg, and Webern—after the violent interruption of World War I is in large part the history of the attempt to transcend the miniature, to integrate the new sense of consonance into a musical language capable of more heroic forms.

The Society for the Private Performance of Music

● ● ●

111

By 1914 Schoenberg had created a style extremely difficult to sustain: a centralized system, tonality, in which everything was ordered by its relation to a fundamental perfect triad, had been replaced by a decentralized system in which cadence or resolution was achieved partly by tone color, rhythm, texture, and phrasing, and partly by the new importance given to chromatic saturation. There was no longer a clear stylistic hierarchy, with everything subordinate to the so-called "rules" of voice-leading (the contrapuntal resolution of harmonic dissonance). Other elements in music now demanded an equal status with pitch. The new style was based on a complex set of equivalences: harmonic dissonance, for example, could now be achieved by means of texture and rhythm.

To some extent these equivalences had always been present in music, but they had been governed by the "laws of harmony," which took precedence. Now that the equivalences were released from this centralized control, the conception of each new work of music required the working out of problems that could no longer be easily schematized. Both result and cause (or *raison d'être*) of the new style was the principle of nonrepetition: equilibrium and resolution were to be achieved without the use of symmetrical repetition. What returned was to be transformed (with the simplest form of transformation, decoration, theoretically excluded)—an admirable principle only for the composition of very short works, so Webern later felt. The outcome was not only a style difficult to sustain, but one that made unprecedented demands upon the listeners.

The war put an almost complete stop to the musical life of Europe: only Stravinsky, working in the security of Switzerland, continued to produce major works. Schoenberg finished only the Four Songs for Orchestra. In 1917, he sketched the oratorio *Die Jakobsleiter*, which makes evident concessions in order to speak clearly, to be more immediately grasped by an audience: many passages imply a central perfect triad; the melodic lines are frequently long and simple; even the gargantuan size of the originally conceived scoring (four hidden orchestras, two hidden choirs, a main choir of seven hundred and twenty in twelve parts, and a principal orchestra with fifty violins and other numerical forces to match) is reminiscent of the *Gurrelieder*. It has much of the dramatic power and the anguish of the music of 1909, and the chromatic texture has a new simplicity that foreshadows the works of the 1920s. It anticipates *Moses und Aron* above all in its use of *Sprechstimme* for choral groups.

Schoenberg was never to finish *Die Jakobsleiter*, and, in fact, he was able to complete nothing more until 1923.

Meanwhile he occupied himself in a direct and original fashion with the deteriorating relation between the contemporary composer and the public. In 1918, he founded the Society for the Private Performance of Music. The Society's prospectus was drafted by Alban Berg, and many of Schoenberg's pupils were active in it. The programs for the concerts, which generally took place on Sunday mornings, were not announced in advance, and there was no publicity. Subscriptions were sold, but subscribers had to pledge not to publish reports about the concerts or to write or solicit criticisms of them. In this way, the performances were to remain "private," withdrawn from commercial stimulus and from the expectation of fame.

The Society was an extension of Schoenberg's teaching; it was, at least in theory, an instrument of education and not of propaganda. Contemporary works were at last rehearsed for as long hours as needed to be played well: music that required more than one performance to be understood was repeated several times at subsequent concerts. The center of interest was to be the music itself, and the performer was relegated firmly to second place. The music was to be protected from the ruinously bad performances that difficult contemporary music generally received because of the organization of concert life, centered upon the standard repertory. Above all, the music was to be withdrawn both from the dictates of fashion, which inflated and deflated reputations arbitrarily, and from the pressures of commercialism.

It was a grandiose and generous scheme. Schoenberg allowed no work of his own to be played for the first year and a half. The initial program consisted of music by

Skryabin, Debussy, and Mahler; during the few years of the Society's life, Debussy and Reger were the composers with the largest numbers of works performed. On three occasions the austere policy of performing only difficult contemporary works was relaxed, in two concerts of Mozart, Beethoven, and Brahms, and an evening of Strauss waltzes.[1] The waltzes, arranged by Schoenberg, Berg, and Webern, were played in May 1921 in order to raise money to keep the Society going. (Standards of performance were as stringent as ever for these evenings: five five-hour rehearsals.) Schoenberg's arrangements were a return to his earliest professional activity: for years he had orchestrated operettas to make a living. (The purely technical professionalism of such an activity should be underscored. Schoenberg, who was playing the violin and composing at the age of eight, is often described as an autodidact because he did not attend a music school —as if composers ever learned much of their trade in such schools anyway, and as if the help he received when he was seventeen from his friend Alexander von Zemlinsky, who *was* attending music school, did not give him all the teaching he needed.)

The Society was created to give contemporary music back to the musicians to whom it belonged, to take it away from the corrupt influence of the public market place. Put this way, it is not an ideal that invites challenge. Nevertheless, the conception of music as an activity that can be so withdrawn, so separated from all other aspects of life is, as a matter of fact, the precipitate of a long tradition of thinking about art in commercial terms. Music, understood as an absolutely separate ac-

[1]These statistics are drawn from Willi Reich, *Schoenberg*, pp. 119–22.

tivity, is a commodity. It belongs to musicians most of all in the sense that it is what they have to sell. Music may be an instinctive part of human life, but the craft of composition and performance transforms this instinct into a separate profession.

This commercialization, which turned the art of music into a clearly defined activity capable of producing ever-new and original works that would render the style of the previous generation out of date—works with built-in obsolescence, in short—this commercialization may be reasonably credited with the extraordinary and rapid development of secular music from Bach to Schoenberg. In order to work, however, the process requires the continuous pretense that what is sold has been made in fact for its own sake, that what society is buying transcends all social utility, or else its value would come crashing down. By 1900, this pretense was subject to strains that were about to tear it apart. High art—conceived in professional and commercial terms—demands that the public refuse to buy whatever has been produced solely for the purpose of consumption, whatever does not come directly out of the artist's inner nature by a kind of necessity. To write specifically for sale what does not come from the heart is a swindle. Writing music that is deliberately accessible, more easily understood, is therefore the ultimate cheat: it is packaging a fake. That is why neglect and misunderstanding came to seem to be a prerequisite for ultimate, commercial success (frequently posthumous).[2] When the claim that the public and the artist wanted the same thing could no longer be maintained, as it could not for some time before World

[2]In an age when even sold-out operatic and symphonic performances must be heavily subsidized, this commercial success is naturally an illusion.

War I, the crisis of the arts that we are so familiar with began. The *Gebrauchsmusik* of the 1920s (music for social use) and Schoenberg's Society for the Private Performance of Music were both solutions of despair: Schoenberg's was the more honorable course.

The hope that once these difficult works were given really fine performance they would become accepted by the public was, oddly, a surrender to the commercialism that Schoenberg so deplored. It is understood, of course, that most performances of new works now as then are a travesty of the scores. Those notes which are not played wrong or which are played at all (when the musicians or conductor have not lost their place) are generally rendered without understanding, without sensibility, and often without simple good will. But it is naïve to think that better executions will have much more chance of success: I have seen performances with two-thirds of the notes wrong or missing greeted with tremendous enthusiasm, and watched subscribers at symphony concerts march out in rage during a ravishing and accurate performance of Berg's delightful short (!) *Post-Card Songs.* The crisis brought on by conceiving of music as a salable commodity is not solved by making it more easily sold or by turning the public into educated buyers. Schoenberg's Society was a solution of despair, but it was (and is) necessary to maintain the ideal that music is performed because musicians wish to write and play it. Better performances do not make difficult music popular, but they keep music alive.

Music is, of course, not strictly a commodity; it is, as I have said, worth buying only when the pretense that it is not a commodity can be successfully maintained. The separation of music from other social activities imposed by the commercial organization of the arts has over the centuries created problems no closer to being solved to-day than in 1919. The attempt to draw on folk music, for example, in order to reintegrate music in the general order of human activities has resulted inevitably in the commercialization of folk music itself: folk kitsch is un-doubtedly the most pervasive form of kitsch ever elabo-rated. In any case, the uneasy relation of composer and public today cannot be solved by composers, who must live with it as best they can: it is the creation of forces far too large for musicians to do anything about.

At the end of 1921, after less than three years of ex-istence, the Society for the Private Performance of Music gave its last concert, and closed down because of the fantastically spiraling inflation of the Austrian cur-rency.

Serialism and Neoclassicism

IV

Schoenberg's most pressing concern, after World War I, was to return to the great central tradition of Western music. Not only had the existence of this civilized tradition been made precarious by the war's devastation, but its coherence had been threatened by the revolutionary developments of the preceding years. The years of Schoenberg's silence, 1918–1923, were years of general despair: the only significant new movement in the arts was the nihilistic Dada, which quickly died after a brilliant display of fireworks.

The problem was, above all, to integrate the advances of 1908–1913 with the inheritance of the eighteenth and nineteenth centuries. When Schoenberg in 1921 privately confided to a friend that his invention of serialism would guarantee the supremacy of German music for centuries to come, his claim is not merely an example of that arrogant Prussian chauvinism characteristic of the non-Prussian citizens of the German border states. The central tradition was, indeed, German, and the rising influence of French and Russian music was as great a menace to its integrity as the innovations of Schoenberg and his school. The aim was to reconstitute and preserve that integrity.

The atmosphere of the 1920s was very different from that of the prewar years: the fashionable luxuriance of Art Nouveau gave way to the equally chic commercial severity of Art Deco. The music of this decade often returned to the language of tonality purified of chromaticism, a return that never succeeded in using tonality as a natural language but always as a quotation, indeed as a sign. The tonic-dominant relations are never neutral now, always filled with significance, ironic and bittersweet in the music of Milhaud and Poulenc, emblematic of middle-class academic achievement in Honegger and Hindemith. Bartók's chromatic expressionism was increasingly deflected by his attempts to reach a modified form of tonality by using the modal systems of central European folk music: in his greatest achievements, however, he kept alive the expressionist style only slightly chastened by his modal researches. Stravinsky alone, treating tonality as if it were an archaic and foreign language, created a genuine and viable neoclassical style *en grand seigneur:* he used nonchromatic tonal relations ruthlessly, disrupting both their harmonic and rhythmic aspects, and made no attempt to create effects of nostalgia or respectability; the opening of his piano sonata, for example, interchanges tonic and dominant (harmonizing a note of the tonic triad with a dominant chord, and vice versa) until their functions are almost obliterated and the tonal hierarchy disappears. Stravinsky's great neoclassical works of the 1920s and 1930s do not rely on the traditional language of tonality; they use and exploit the elements of tonality according to an elegant set of new rules.

Neoclassicism and serialism (or twelve-tone music) are often considered polar opposites. The enmity between Vienna and Paris, between the school of Schoenberg and the school of Stravinsky, is a fact of history. (In passing, it may be noted that the school of Nadia Boulanger would be a better name than the school of Stravinsky for those innumerable composers who went to study in Paris. Stravinsky declined all educational responsibilities, and they were assumed, committedly in his interest, by Mlle. Boulanger.) This opposition has long since broken down: not only have the two "schools" drawn closer together, but their differences—even at the height of the crossfire in the late 1920s—no longer seem significant. The similarities between Stravinsky's *Jeu de Cartes* and Schoenberg's Quartet, opus 30, with their imitations of early-nineteenth-century form and phrasing, between large religious works such as *Die Jakobsleiter* (or parts of *Moses und Aron*) and the *Symphony of Psalms,* have become more apparent. These were parallel rather than opposing movements, and the ease with which composers such as Aaron Copland combined both styles has shown how compatible they were after all.

One often hears a weightless charge: that there is an opposition within Schoenberg's own music between his serialist technique and his openly neoclassical forms. There is no question that the conservative tendencies in Schoenberg's style increased and even hypertrophied with the appearance of serialism. The forms are often simpler and more symmetrical; even the instrumentation is more conventional; the orchestral forces are less extravagant.

Nevertheless, whatever aesthetic contradictions may have been gradually uncovered between serialism and the standard nineteenth-century forms, Schoenberg was not a radical inventor who withdrew into conservatism after his creation of the twelve-tone system. He may have misjudged the potentiality of his own thought, but the invention of serialism was specifically a move to resurrect an old classicism as well as to make a new one possible. Moreover, serialism developed step by step from some of the most traditional features of Western music.

The works that represent the turning point are opus 23, 24, and 25, with which Schoenberg broke the silence of many years. (The opus numbers do not reflect the order of composition. Each work is made up of at least five pieces, written and reworked at various times between 1920 and 1923. For example, opus 24 no. 1 was begun on August 3, 1920; the Prelude of opus 25 is dated July 24, 1921; and opus 23 no. 4 was begun on July 26, 1921, and finished on February 13, 1923.[1]) It was in these sets of pieces that serial technique was elaborated, but what must be emphasized is the consanguinity of the pages of nonserial music and those in strict twelve-tone form.

The Five Piano Pieces, opus 23, show this clearly. Only the fifth piece, a waltz, is strictly serial, yet the other four are written in a style that approximates serialism closely

[1]See Josef Rufer, *The Works of Arnold Schoenberg* (London, 1962).

and in some respects represent serial procedures better. All five pieces are governed by two long-familiar principles of composition: the principle of the unity of musical material, and the principle of motivic development and variation. From these two is derived—by extension and systemization—the technique of twelve-tone composition. These principles were expanded to fill the void left by the disappearance of tonality and to take over its functions. Their power to expand, which gives them the status of a system, rests on the tendency of chromatic music to fill chromatic space.

By the middle of the second measure of opus 23 no. 1, nine notes of the chromatic scale have been played, none of them twice; the three remaining notes follow before the end of the next measure. Two cellular motifs govern these opening measures completely and dominate much of what follows:

and

The two cells are closely related: each is made up of a minor second and a minor third. The textures are thin and transparent. The old six-note chords of 1908–1913 are gone: the writing is in only three, or sometimes four, distinct voices.

The character is that of a Brahms intermezzo, the form almost as simple. An opening section, with a melody built from the two cells, is followed by a new melody, lighter in character (although a little slower) and made from similar material—minor seconds and thirds giving way to major seconds and thirds; then the two melodies are combined. The combination is enlivened by a sensitive, learned, and continuously shifting use of the traditional variation techniques of imitation, augmentation, diminution, inversion, retrograde motion, and octave transposition.[2]

The classical distinction between melody and accompaniment—which may tend to disappear if the accompanying voices are derived directly from the same material as the melody—is rigidly enforced by the dynamics. In measure 29, for example, the main theme is marked *piano:* the echoes of this, twice and four times as fast, are marked *pianissimo,* and the accompanying figure derived from the second theme is ppp, or *pianississimo.* Schoenberg never abandoned this hierarchy of principal and subordinate voices.

The third piece of opus 23 is even more intensively derived from a single motif, a five-note theme played without accompaniment at the opening. Here the presentation suggests a fugal answer, as the second voice enters directly after the first—even, in fact, before it has finished—at the fourth below. (As in the first piece, nine notes of the chromatic scale are introduced at once before any is repeated, and the remaining three follow without delay.) Almost all the accompanying figures as well as the main voices spring from the opening motif, and it creates the harmonic character of the piece by its combination chords as well.

From this method of motivic development filling all the chromatic space almost immediately, it is only a small step to the strict serial technique of opus 23 no. 5. In this waltz, the motif has twelve notes and now covers all the notes of the chromatic scale. The principle of derivation has been made absolutely rigorous: every note of the piece, accompanying voice or main part, comes

[2]Octave transposition is the shifting of one or more notes of a melody to a higher or lower register.

from the twelve-note motif. The order of the notes within the motif—which may now be called a "series"—has also been made rigorous: few liberties are taken with the order fixed at the opening.

The waltz is, however, a timid step toward serialism: the series appears at first as a melody. The order of notes from which the rest of the piece is to be constructed is presented in the highest voice: accompanying the first four notes, the left hand—with a *pianissimo* to mark its subordination—plays notes six through twelve of the series, and then goes on to play one through five as the right hand completes the full statement in the correct order.[3] Until measure 104 (out of 112), the order is always one through twelve: at this one place it is played backward. Not only is the original order preserved except this once,[4] but there are no transpositions and no inversions. In this respect the motivic technique is less sophisticated than that of the nonserial pieces of opus 23, where transposition, inversion, and regroupings are much more freely used.

Everything in this piece depends on three kinds of variation: different rhythmic groupings (and the dynamics implied by these), octave displacement (playing two contiguous notes of the series in different registers), and chordal groupings (playing several contiguous notes simultaneously instead of one after the other as they are first presented). While the chordal groups allow for the effect of harmony, it is upon the rhythm, dynamics, and texture that the main burden for the variety and development of the music lies. It is above all the rhythm that

[3]At a few points one note or a small group of notes is taken out of order, generally in an accompanying figure.
[4]When these chords are rolled, i.e., arpeggiated, a minimal change in the order of the series is introduced.

establishes the character of the piece, which is that of the typical Viennese waltz, sentimental charm and all, in absolutely everything but harmony. Even the occasional 4/8 measure is present in homage to the traditionally exaggerated *rubato* that the style demands.

This waltz is generally credited with being the first twelve-tone piece: it represents, in fact, very little of twelve-tone technique or even of its aesthetic. The main interest is concentrated on the ingenious problem: how many different and striking rhythmic groups can be made using only one fixed sequence of twelve notes? The other pieces of opus 23 are more indicative of the future in the way their motifs are transformed by inversion and transposed freely so that they may start on any note. Even the fixed order of the twelve notes in the waltz is a misleading model on which to base an idea of serial music, which does not, in fact, demand that the order of notes be consistently and monotonously identical in each phrase.

There is, however, one revolutionary aspect about this piece. The waltz breaks open the previous aesthetic with great consequences for the future by its nonmelodic conception of the basic motif or set: except at the beginning, the order of twelve notes is not a melody, but a quarry for melodies; the melodic line may at times start in the middle of one presentation of the set and continue part of the way into the next. In the other pieces in opus 23, the motif usually has a clearly perceptible integrity, a shape with a beginning and an end. In the waltz, the phrases are broken without regard to the twelve-note set, which has an identifiable shape of its own only the first time it is played.

The contradictions that are found in opus 23 reappear in the Serenade for clarinet, basset-horn, mandoline, guitar, violin, viola, violoncello, and a deep male voice, opus 24. Here the fourth movement, a setting of Petrarch's Sonnet no. 217, may be called strict twelve-tone. The singer repeats the same twelve notes twelve times; but since a line of Petrarch has only eleven syllables, each successive verse begins one note earlier in the twelve-note series and has a different melodic configuration. The series is therefore not a melody but a premelodic idea, used to furnish the stuff of melody. This is not new: both Beethoven and Brahms used motifs this way, but neither had conceived of a set of pitches as entirely divorced from their rhythmic and harmonic implications. The motif, which has always a specific contour, a profile, in becoming a series loses this attribute of shape. The series is not a musical idea in the normal sense of that phrase. It is not properly speaking something heard, either imaginatively or practically; it is transmuted into something heard.

The motif, on the other hand, is an idea heard, and Schoenberg's development of motivic material in other pieces of the Serenade is remarkably sophisticated, particularly when compared with the simple-minded, obsessive repetitions of the Petrarch sonnet. In most of the Serenade, this complex motivic elaboration and an atonal language are put to work in the re-creation of late eighteenth- and early nineteenth-century phrasing. The evocation of the elegant surface of the past was by 1923 as much a part of Schoenberg's music as of Strauss's (in *Ariadne auf Naxos*) or Stravinsky's (in *Pulcinella and L'Histoire d'un soldat*). A high price was set on charm. The ostensibly light character of the Serenade, opus 24, is still a stumbling block in appreciating its merits; its high gloss can awaken resentment. There is no contradiction, however, between its highly experimental character—its technical adventurousness, in fact—and the bland efficiency with which it turns back to the past. The experiments are designed to recapture the security of a vanished classicism; the smoothness of surface is a measure of their success.

The third set of short pieces which Schoenberg composed during the early 1920s, the Suite for Piano, opus 25, is the real landmark. If parts of it were written before the waltz, as has been conjectured,[5] it is all the more astonishing. In this work, we have not only a fixed order for the twelve tones, as we found in the waltz; in addition, the concept of the transformations essential to serial music is already considerably developed. Moreover, all the dances in the Suite are composed from the same twelve-tone series; not only is Schoenberg's avowed purpose of unity achieved, but the suppleness and capabilities of the new serial method are demonstrated.

The dances are those of the standard Baroque suite, except for a central intermezzo—a romantic meditation of almost Brahmsian character, similar to those of opus 23—and once again the commanding reference to the past is not fortuitous. If serialism was to be not a break with tradition but a bridge from the incontrovertible accomplishments of the great atonal period into the center of history once again, it was important in this first completely serial work to demonstrate how it could deal with the basic classical forms: the final proof was to be the facility and charm with which these forms were reanimated.

The essential elements of Schoenberg's serialism are all present in the Suite, opus 25. The twelve tones are arranged in a fixed order:

[5]By Rufer, *op. cit.,* p. 45.

H C A B = BACH reversed

(The order in this piece falls naturally into three groups, articulated by an augmented fourth, or tritone, symmetrically placed at the end of the first and second groups.) The series may be played in its original form and backward (retrograde form); it may also be inverted, and the inversion played backward. These are the four primary manifestations of the series: theoretically the original form has no primacy over the retrograde, the inversion, and the retrograde inversion. The series chosen for opus 25 has an unusual feature, as the inversion of its first four notes reproduces the tritone of the third and fourth notes (G and C-sharp) exactly reversed:

Original form

Inversion

All four forms of the series may be transposed, i.e., played starting on any other note. The only transposition that Schoenberg uses in opus 25 is an augmented fourth, in order to take advantage of the character of this particular series, which begins on an E and ends on a B-flat, a tritone apart. In this way both the retrograde form of the original series and the transposed form begin with the same note. Furthermore, the only transposed form of the first four notes reproduces the tritone C-sharp–G exactly reversed, as does the inversion.

The transposed form, too, begins on a B-flat and ends on an E, reversing the beginning and end of the original

Original form

Transposition

form. These correspondences all arise from the symmetrical nature of the tritone: it is exactly the midpoint of the octave. In this work, therefore, the tritone has become the most important interval: it appears twice within the series and frames it at its outer limits. This suggests the basic rule of Schoenberg's serial aesthetic: the large form of a piece—its transformations and developments—should arise from the character of the particular series chosen. It was not a rule that he himself was later able to accept without considerable (if unspoken) reservations.

Further transformations of the series are possible, when it is divided (or partitioned) into two or more groups. One part of the series may be played with another as long as the integrity of the inner group is retained. The integrity of the group is a guarantee of the identity of the motif, which remains consistently recognizable. In Schoenberg's own practice, these transformations reveal the ambiguity of his concept of serialism: the series was, for him, both a group of motifs and an organization of the tonal spectrum. In other words, the series was at one and the same time a means of deriving melodic lines through transformation of motifs, and a coherent framework whose structural functions could replace those of tonality. Only to a certain extent did these aspects coincide; at times they were almost in direct opposition.

One further essential point of the grammar of serialism remains to be mentioned: the role of the octave. It is not true (although it is still sometimes claimed) that octaves are taboo in serial music: they may be used as doublings. Schoenberg avoided octave doubling in the first years of his serial composition but made considerable use of it later. What must be avoided are octaves that result from the collision of two different forms of the series. In other words, one of the series' four basic forms must not be combined with another (or with a transposition) in such a way as to create a momentary octave. It is the octaves that come from two separate voices that cause a disturbance. This is because of the constitution of the series.

Serial music systematizes what I have called the weak form of chromatic saturation: it acknowledges the tyranny of the octave as absolute. The series, in fact, is not an order of pitches but of what is called pitch-classes. For example, in the first two notes of the series of opus 25 quoted above, as long as some E, high or low, is followed by any F, the serial conditions are satisfied. Tonal music had gone only part of the way to asserting the equivalence of all octaves, but Schoenberg's serialism went much further, and made it the structural foundation of his music.

Speculations have recently arisen on the possibility of writing music with some module other than the octave —that is, of refusing to treat all F's, F-sharps, etcetera, as in any sense identical. Since the octave is the most powerful harmonic, it is naturally present as a powerful acoustic force in every note *when played:* in this sense it is at least partially identifiable with the note. Nevertheless, musical systems are constituted to disregard certain acoustical facts while exploiting others. Electronic music can reduce the component of the octave harmonic (although the acoustics of a room in which an electronically produced tape is played will go a little way to restoring it). It is, at any rate, ironic to note, in light of the virulent attacks made on Schoenberg's system as unnatural, that no composer has ever submitted with as much humility to this force of nature as he.

Since serialism is an organization of all the octave-classes, the presence of an octave when each note comes from a distinct, separate version of the series creates generally an unacceptable confusion. It threatens the method of organization itself, occasions a mistake in grammar so serious as to destroy sense. The prohibition of such octaves is part of a larger principle of nonredundancy. This does not ban the repetition of a note. What it bans is the return of a note in such a context as to imply the disruption of the series. For example, the first note of one form of a series may be repeated as often as a composer likes, provided it always sounds like the first note (in other words, as though the note was sustained with intermittences); it must not sound as if it had a second position in the series.

The principle of nonredundancy implies and clarifies the nonmotivic aspect of the series. There is no reason why a note (or one of its octave transpositions) should not have two places in a motif. But a note that occurs at two separate points of a motif will generally have a different function each time—it may move in a different direction, close or open a smaller part of the motif. The function of a note in a series, however, is almost entirely dependent on its position relative to the other eleven notes. Schoenberg's serialism poses as its initial condition the homogeneity of chromatic space. Each pitch is theoretically as important as every other one, and it can have no intrinsic importance that places it above another; *it cannot act except through its place in the series.* The principle of nonredundancy simply implies that the relative positions within the series must be respected.

This homogeneity was not, in fact, completely congenial to Schoenberg: from the beginning he attempted to undercut it by his choice of transpositions. As we have seen above, the only transposition allowed in the Suite, opus 25, has the effect of emphasizing the tritone G–C-sharp, already singled out by the inversion, as well as the tritone B-flat–E, which comes from the first and last notes of the series. In order to set certain elements of the series into relief, Schoenberg is guardedly selective with his transpositions, and deliberately limits the possibilities of serial treatment. With the four basic versions each transposable to eleven notes of the chromatic scale, there are always forty-eight versions available. Schoenberg generally uses only a tiny fraction of these.

By partitioning the series into well-defined motifs and by using transpositions to bring the character of the motifs into sharp relief, many of the functions of tonality could be reconstructed within serialism. The third motif into which the series of opus 25 divides is designed for such a purpose:

The iconographic symbolism of the retrograde form has not been lost on commentators: This motif played backward spells the familiar B–A–C–H (in the German lettering of the notes, in which H is our B and B is our B-flat). Musically more to the point is the aptitude of the motif to imply a resolution on B-flat. This aptitude is reinforced by Schoenberg's decision to allow only the tritone transposition; of the eight versions of the series that appear in opus 25 (four basic forms, each with their tritone transpositions), four begin on B-flat and four end on B-flat.

The other note set similarly into relief is the tritone complement of B-flat–E; and E accordingly is set up as a polar opposite of B-flat throughout the Suite. Part of the polarization of tonic and dominant in tonality is thereby reproduced, although tonal implications are strictly kept at bay, since the tritone is the interval most destructive of a proper sense of key. Nevertheless, the rising seconds of the reversed B–A–C–H motif almost inevitably imply the cadential movement of tonal music, and this motif is accordingly used throughout with the rhythm and phrasing of an eighteenth-century cadence. The motif lends itself credibly to a graceful lilt, and in its limited space seems like a resolution of the tritones in the first two motifs (quoted above, page 80). And it is above all by this means that Schoenberg transmutes the gavotte and the minuet into a modern idiom.

The reconstitution of tonal effects by means of serialism has seemed to many an unrewarding, even an ignoble task. It was taken with the deepest seriousness by Schoenberg and Berg. By his choice of series, and an artful use of transpositions, Berg succeeded in playing the opening of the Prelude to *Tristan und Isolde* in the middle of his Lyric Suite for string quartet, as well as a Bach chorale in his violin concerto. Of course, serial technique is a tiresomely ingenious and time-consuming way of composing Bach and Wagner: but the relevance of the new technique to the great German tradition had to be displayed, its ability to encompass—even textually, if need be—the forms of tonal music. Only when this had been accomplished, it seemed, could one go on to the forms that grew specifically out of serialism alone.

The separation of form and style (or technique) does not begin with Schoenberg: it was as much a part of his inheritance as academic counterpoint or tonal harmony. It was far more difficult to shake off, however, and it was responsible, in later years, for a radical misunderstanding on his part of his own achievements of the expressionist years of 1908–1913. To the end of his life, he persisted in believing that the works of those years— *Erwartung,* the Five Pieces for Orchestra, the Four Orchestral Songs, opus 22—had not achieved a purely musical form drawn from the logic of a purely musical material; they were dependent on extra-musical material, poetical texts, inner feelings, as if these feelings could in the final result be distinguished from their extraordinary musical incarnation. In a revealing remark about the Four Orchestral Songs, Schoenberg confessed that he knew that they had a musical logic of their own but was as yet unable to demonstrate it rationally. He could only sense it.

Form was, for Schoenberg, basically what it was for the nineteenth century: an ideal set of proportions and shapes which transcended style and language. These ideal shapes could be realized at any time in any style; they were absolute. The three great types of form were the sonata, the variation, and the *da capo* form.

Schoenberg's acceptance, at least for all practical purposes, of this conventional view is the more astonishing in that perhaps more than any other musician of his generation, he understood how the classical forms, especially the sonata, were bound up with tonality. The symmetries of the sonata were related to the symmetrical organization of the grammar of tonality, its sense of movement tied to the need for resolution into the tonic triad. With this knowledge, his attempts to reproduce the sonata in an atonal form by means of serialism may seem at first a self-destructive endeavor.

In this re-creation of classical forms within atonality, he was not only followed by his pupil Alban Berg, but actually preceded by him. Berg's Three Pieces for Orchestra of 1913–1914 contain the first example on a large scale of the heroic effort to write an atonal sonata. *Wozzeck* shows throughout a determined use of traditional forms: sonata, suite, fugue, passacaglia, variation, rondo, chorale, scherzo with trio, etcetera. For most of *Wozzeck,* too, tonality is present only as an occasional force, an exceptional contrast to the general atonal structure. These forms are by no means freely interpreted, but arrayed in the full glory of nineteenth-century academicism. They do not arise as a natural expression of the dramatic action, but are impressed upon the drama in an attempt to order what Berg feared would otherwise be amorphous.

That Berg preceded Schoenberg in the employment of traditional large-scale forms (there are a few traditional patterns in *Pierrot Lunaire,* but only in miniature) is an indication that this project was not an idiosyncratic or personal inclination but a tendency of the period: Berg, a generation younger than Schoenberg, found more quickly and with greater ease than Schoenberg the essential characteristics of the decades to come, of the 1920s when Berg reached full artistic maturity. His neoclassicism was immediate and instinctive: Schoenberg's, on the other hand, was laboriously planned and demanded the renunciation of some of his most characteristic talents.

There is an important contrast between Berg's and Schoenberg's attitude to the use of traditional forms.

Berg claimed that he did not want the public to be aware of these forms: Schoenberg, who wished the public to remain unaware of the serial technique, was concerned that the outer forms themselves should be very clearly audible. There is a distinction to be made, of course: Berg's statement is about the employment of academic forms—the "forms of pure music," as he called them—in opera, and he wished the attention concentrated on the dramatic effects. The forms of his chamber music are equally traditional, but neither here nor in the operas are the forms the principal means of conveying the expressive weight. In his chamber music and in his violin concerto as well, the classical forms are neutral organizing principles. They act as molds to contain material whose shape is less important than its ferment, its action upon the physiology of the listener. For Schoenberg, on the contrary, the forms are not imposed on the music, but realized through it: they are, in a sense, to be identified with the expression. Schoenberg, steeped in tonality and still in love with it, used these forms as if they had innate expressive properties.

If these properties, Schoenberg must have thought, were being lost through degenerate pseudo-tonal procedures, they could be restored by serialism. In the late 1920s, he labored chiefly to accomplish this restoration, above all in the Wind Quintet, opus 26; the Suite, opus 29 (for piccolo clarinet, clarinet, bass clarinet, violin, viola, cello, and piano); the String Quartet no. 3, opus 30; and the Variations for Orchestra, opus 31, all written between 1925 and 1928. In these pieces, along with the Suite for Piano, opus 25, we find the extreme points of Schoenberg's neoclassicism.

The most ambitious and in some ways the most fully achieved of these works is the String Quartet no. 3, which Schoenberg modeled on the famous String Quartet in A minor of Schubert. His taking a specific work as a paradigm, and using it as a form to be filled with a new content that is intended in no way to recall the older work, was itself a revival of an earlier practice, most notably that of Schubert and Brahms; it is the fundamental classicistic procedure. What especially interested Schoenberg about the Schubert quartet was its technique of development, as well as—most important of all—its combination of long, sustained melody with a continuously moving accompaniment. In this work (as in others of this period) Schoenberg insisted upon one transposition of the series, that of a fifth down. The relation of the fifth is drawn from the series invented for the work, which contains two successive fifths and another slightly later. The transposition is used to characterize the second theme of the "sonata" form, and there is even a preparation of the "modulation," or a simulation of this traditional effect of tonal music, through the use of the retrograde version of the first five notes of the transposition already heard in the cello in measure 16: it follows these notes in the original pitch, creating a mirror tonic-dominant contrast in the principal melodic part.

There are two basic kinds of relationships in serial music that enabled Schoenberg to realize his neoclassical program. The first is the inner symmetry of a series. The row composed for the Quartet no. 3 shows this easily:

Each half of the row (or each hexachord) contains a minor third, a fifth, and an augmented fourth. This allows for a succession of small-scale symmetries. On the first page of the quartet, for example, the first five notes are played as a steady eight-note accompaniment against the last five notes in the first violin as a lyrical melody.[6] The minor third and tritone in melody and accompaniment reflect each other and create an analogue of the opening of the Schubert quartet, where the steady eighth-note accompaniment and the melody in the first violin are built of the same material, reflecting each other freely.

The second kind of relationship is on a larger scale, and requires the invention of a special kind of series. The series of the Variations for Orchestra, opus 31, is an example:

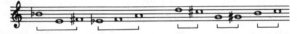

The obvious inner relationships, which I have marked by brackets, lie within the hexachords. The first hexachord contains two groups of three notes, each defining the same chord as the other transposed when the three notes are played together. The possibilities of harmonic parallelism are evident, and accordingly used throughout the work, as are the obvious symmetries of minor seconds in the second hexachord.

But this series has a more important property, which we can see when we arrange the notes of the two hexachords in ascending and descending order:

[6]The middle two notes are assigned to the bass, where they appear as an expressive imitation of the minor second that occurs between notes eight and nine.

One hexachord in clearly the exact inversion of the other transposed. This means that when the original order of the notes in the hexachords is restored, a transposition must exist that will transform all notes in the first hexachord inverted into the pitches of the second hexachord in a different order (and vice versa); the transposition is a minor third down from the one beginning on B-flat quoted above:

This is not an inner relationship but one between different versions of the same series, and is called (following Milton Babbitt) "combinatoriality."

After 1930, Schoenberg was concerned in his serial works to compose music with series having this property. It gave him a rich and easily perceptible set of effects with wide expressive possibilities. Combinatoriality allows the same few pitches to be given very different shapes, while the noncombinatorial transpositions allow the same shapes at different pitches. The stylistic range was considerably enlarged.

After composing the group of works in which the essential lines of his twelve-tone system were laid down, Schoenberg was forced to leave Germany and emigrate, first, briefly, to Spain and then to America. The change was a difficult one for him. Eventually in 1934 he settled, like Stravinsky, in Hollywood; he taught at the University of California until 1944 and continued to teach privately after that until his death on July 13, 1951. He was one of the greatest teachers of the century: most of his instruction was of the traditional tonal disciplines, harmony and counterpoint. No one has ever insisted more upon a thorough mastery of traditions as a basis for original work: he was concerned that the music of the past be retained both as a living craft with its own identity and by integration into the new.

In the American years, Schoenberg not only tried to find serial equivalents for tonal structures but experimented with the absorption of purely tonal effects into serialism. In the piano concerto composed in 1942, he employed octave doublings, which gave him the typical virtuoso sonority associated with the genre: the lyricism he sought (and achieved) in parts of this work is clearly a remembrance of nineteenth-century textures. He wrote a number of tonal works in this last period, or, at least, works that to some extent make use of the functions of tonic and dominant and in which the harmony is largely triadic. These works bear the unmistakable stamp of Schoenberg's personal manner, but he felt understandably defensive about them: they were exercises in virtuosity, he explained, and signified no repudiation of his serial work.

Even more important than these "tonal" exercises in the later works was his choice (or invention) of twelve-tone rows of a kind he had previously avoided—those which outline perfect triads and which lend themselves to the momentary suggestion of tonal effects. In this he had once more been anticipated by Berg. The contrast of major and minor at certain exceptional moments was an effect that the younger composer was reluctant to abandon, because of its powerful expressive possibilities; these "tonal" moments occur at crucial points both in *Lulu* and in Berg's violin concerto. In Schoenberg's String Quartet no. 4, opus 37 (1936), and the *Ode to Napoleon,* opus 41 (1942), most notably, the underlying row is so constructed as to facilitate the use of perfect triads. No amount of emphasis on an E-flat-major triad will ever, indeed, be sufficient to establish the key of E-flat major; and the *Ode to Napoleon* is no more in E-flat than it is in F-sharp: the E-flat triads are a deliberate quotation, a reference to that other great "Napoleonic" work the *Eroica* Symphony. In the Quartet no. 4 and the *Ode,* the use of perfect triads is as much a defiant proclamation of freedom as an exercise in nostalgia.

The neoclassical program is a paradoxical one. The reappearance of elements of tonality in a completely serialized context preserves only the similitude of these elements while destroying their original significance. They gain a new significance, but the goal has changed from preservation into complete transmutation. In this sense, neither Berg nor Schoenberg were conservative, but radical reactionaries.

Their program has been repudiated today. This does not, of course, touch the validity of the music they wrote. In the attempt to realize their program, too, they elaborated techniques that are now put to a very different use. Much of the suppleness of contemporary serial music was already developed by Schoenberg and Berg: their extraordinary successes notwithstanding, the attempt to find a bridge to the past was a test of the powers of serialism, less a false route than an indispensable initial step.

Two works written by Schoenberg after the invention of serialism have a special place. The first dates from just before Schoenberg's departure for America in October 1933: the first two acts of the opera *Moses und Aron* (the third was never written) were composed between 1930 and 1932. Of all Schoenberg's later works, it is the most immediately convincing to the general public. This is not due to the dramatic interest of a stage production:

on the contrary, concert performances are even more effective. The libretto, written by Schoenberg himself, cannot be taken seriously as literature, but its power of inspiring and reinforcing the music is undeniable. One aspect of the opera is clearly autobiographical in intention. The inarticulate Moses, whose mystical vision of God cannot be translated into song, and the voluble Aron, whose view of God is entirely in terms of outward signs and miracles, are part of an allegory whose subject is the impossibility of realizing an artistic vision.

All the music of this immense work is drawn from the transformations of a single series: it is the triumph of Schoenberg's ideal of drawing a wealth of themes from a single source. The series is no longer conceived in any way as melodic, but the main interest still lies in the creation of melodies. The same elements recur in an incredible variety of shapes; the large-scale form is determined most of all by the succession of themes, characteristic and identifiable. Except for an academic orgy around the Golden Calf, with hopelessly square rhythms, Schoenberg's imagination was at its most inventive. The use of *Sprechstimme* is perhaps more effective than anywhere else in Schoenberg, particularly in the opening scene, unique in its use of the timbre of a small chorus. The tone color of this and other episodes transcends the purely thematic conception of the form.

One other work rejoins the expressionist style at moments in its vivid use of instrumental timbre, the marvelous String Trio, opus 45, of 1946. On August 2, 1946, after a violent attack of asthma, Schoenberg's heart stopped beating: he was revived, but it took almost three weeks for him to recover. On August 20 he began writing the trio as a memorial to his own momentary death; it was finished by September 23. Written at great speed, it is a synthesis of much of Schoenberg's music, bringing together aspects that do not often coexist in the same work. Like many of his later works, it is based on a series that permits the introduction of the perfect triads associated with tonality, although it avoids any implication of the harmonic function of tonality. Schoenberg uses these perfect triads for what might be called their latent aspects of sweetness and repose, but he avoids using them for any sense of cadence; they initiate but do not close. To what an extent these latent qualities are naturally inherent in the triads and to what extent culturally induced is not an answerable puzzle: the purity of the harmonic series in these chords plays an evident role, and so does their traditional association with the structural consonances of tonal music. Schoenberg uses the triads as a background for his most expressive motifs, and he does not rely on the "innate" potency of the triads to make his point, which is always clarified essentially by texture. Schoenberg exploits the triads here, but he does not (as Berg does in his last works) rely on them.

The form of this trio is an astonishing synthesis of neoclassicism and chromatic expressionism: the reminiscences of the earlier style are particularly impressive. There are three sections, and the third is an almost academic recapitulation of the first (the use of inversion and the rescoring do not alter the sense of an exact return), but the texture and phrasing are fragmentary; the search for classical continuity has been abandoned, along with any significant attempt at representing the neoclassical alternation of principal themes and transitional motifs. The division into small contrasting fragments, out of whose succession alone arises a convincing sense of movement, as in *Erwartung,* is a return to the years before World War I. (After the invention of serialism, only the remarkable Music for a Film Sequence, opus 34, of 1929–1930, shows a similar independence of nineteenth-century schemata.) The fragmentary units of the trio, however, attain a balance and equilibrium clearly derived from the experiments with classical form: it is a delicately nuanced equilibrium, and there is no question of attempting an absolute musical symmetry.

Serialism appeared to realize an old dream of classical musical aesthetics: the reconciliation of unity and diversity. The unity is guaranteed by the series, which retains an essential invariance through all its forty-eight incarnations. Out of the series, an extraordinary variety of melodic and rhythmic shapes could be drawn. The purpose of serialism was to set the composer's imagination free to create diversity: the abiding unity was to be a lesser matter of concern.

But the aesthetics of Schoenberg's serialism brought serious consequences. In one respect, it was a grave step backward from the vision of his early work, when he had seen that timbre, tone color, and texture were not merely accessories but could be as fundamental to music as pitch. Schoenberg's twelve-tone system once again exalted pitch as the essential vehicle of invariance, as the fundamental element of unity. It did so, however, at one remove—and that is its grandeur. In theory (although Schoenberg's practice never really followed the theory), the set of pitches of the "original" form of the series had no pre-eminence over the forty-seven other sets.

In serialism as Schoenberg conceived it, it is not pitch itself that becomes tyrannical, but intervallic relations. Through all the transformations of the row, the intervallic relations remain absolutely unchanged, pre-empting all relationships of rhythm, dynamics, and timbre. Moreover, in an important sense, these basic intervallic relations find no substitute in serialism for the harmonic structure of tonality to make them more efficient: they must guarantee their own efficiency. The identity of complementary intervals (thirds and sixths, fourths and fifths, sevenths and seconds, unisons and octaves) reveals this clearly. These are complementary because they fill out the octave and use the same notes: A over G is a second, G over A a seventh (the identity of seconds and sevenths must naturally be extended to all octave transpositions of one member of the interval—i.e., ninths, fourteenths, sixteenths, etcetera).

In tonal music, these intervals are identical only insofar as their significance is harmonic rather than motivic: the harmonic significance is never entirely absent, of course, but other aspects retain considerable independence. (A fourth and its complementary inversion, a fifth, are, even with no accompanying bass, opposed in their function, the former being a dissonance, the latter a consonance.) The identity is therefore insured only by their harmonic role.

In Schoenberg's serialism, however, the motivic and harmonic aspects have only atavistic vestiges of independence. The first two notes of the series of *Moses und Aron,* A and B-flat, may be either a second, seventh, ninth, fourteenth, sixteenth, and so forth. Schoenberg's own practice does not, in fact, distinguish between these very different intervals even motivically except in a very localized sense. They retain their characteristic integrity only for a brief moment, generally no longer than that of the individual phrase. Outside this range, we cannot say that Schoenberg makes absolutely no distinction between seconds and sevenths, but the basis of his distinction is less motivic than textural. The motive can be adequately realized either in the serried texture of a second or the open texture of a seventh, and is not primarily tied to one or another form. This is true of Schoenberg's serialism from the beginning, and it is part of the essential decentralization that came with the end of tonality. A motif that contains, for example, A and B-flat no longer has a primary form that must be either a second or a seventh: any one of the various intervals formed by an A and a B-flat, and all possible transpositions of all these intervals, now have theoretically an equally central position. This leaves an extraordinary freedom in realizing the motif, but it is still a system with only one aspect of music that has a fundamental structural function: pitch, whose tyranny (against which Schoenberg himself eloquently protested) is thereby reaffirmed more securely than ever.

This tyranny can be circumvented. In Schoenberg's own style, the character of each work is given less by the series than by the rhythmic movement, which is not so much related to the series as forced upon it. The rhythmic texture of late Schoenberg, and the phrasing and dynamics that depend upon it, were always those of nineteenth-century tonality.

The cause of this dichotomy between serial organization and tonal phrasing lies deeper than an attempt to salvage the past. It comes directly from Schoenberg's view of the double nature of the tone row, motivic and constructive: as a quarry for motifs, and at the same time as a means of organizing the large-scale form. These two aspects of the series, microscopic and macroscopic respectively, were difficult for Schoenberg to bring together. What prevented a synthesis (although it did not

prevent great music of a very eccentric kind) was paradoxically that these two aspects were seen by Schoenberg obstinately as governed by the same principle: the
invention and variation of themes. Like Alban Berg, in
the words quoted on page 34, he believed that "the
melody, the principal part, the theme, is the basis of
[serial], as of all other, music." The use of so many synonyms ("melody," "principal part," "theme") gives just
cause for the suspicion that what Berg means is not so
straightforward as it might appear. In fact, what Berg
means by theme is not what most musicians would
mean by melody.

Form was as basically thematic for Schoenberg as it
had been for most nineteenth-century composers. The
shape of a work for them was primarily determined by
the order and variety of the themes. The ambiguity in
this conception, revealed in Berg's synonyms and in the
aggressiveness of his assertion, had already appeared
more than a hundred years before: an ambiguous, continuously shifting, undefined area reaches from "motif"
to "melody," with "theme" as a neutral, uncommitted
go-between. The relation of motif to melody was already
problematic in Beethoven and Wagner, and made possible the absurd claim that both composers lacked melodic
invention.

Neither melody nor motif is a simple linear succession. "Motif" is a succession, generally short, with a latent power of development, of variation, of creating a
larger continuity. "Melody" is a definable shape, an ara-
besque with a quasi-dramatic structure of tension and
resolution. These definitions contain, however, a hidden
implication: both motif and melody are *tonal* forms. The
power of development and variation that lies in a motif
is given by the context of tonality, above all by the func-

tions of dissonance and consonance: it is this that allows a motif to imply movement, that gives it a propulsive force. The structure of melody is equally tonal: a melody is intended above all to be memorable, and its mnemonic powers comes from the adherence of its line to tonal functions. The sense of sustained line in melody depends on the sustaining of dissonance, the approach to, and temporary withholding of, resolution: this is the source of its expressive power. The sense of dissonance and resolution cannot properly be drawn out of serialism, but must be imposed upon it.

Schoenberg's music is among the most expressive ever written. The expressive motif is fundamental to it. Even in *Erwartung,* where the motif does not determine the large form, it dominates each small section. Schoenberg never renounced a conception of form in which the expressive motif or melody took the central role. This is the basis of his neoclassicism. Serial technique was invented to sustain this expressivity when tonality had grown so weak and so diffuse that it could produce only melodic lines as flaccid and as accommodating as those of Rachmaninov, Pfitzner, and Fauré. By its toughness, serialism restored expressivity at first—literally by being so difficult to use for that purpose. The attempt to create "melodies" against the grain of serialism restored the necessary tension that had gone out of tonality.

Motif generates melody: that is the traditional relation between them. Nevertheless, the generative powers of a motif means that it already contains a melodic structure in miniature. In Bach and in the Viennese classics, three or four notes contain the structure of dissonance-consonance and so sound as a memorable, self-contained unit. Beethoven, one of the greatest melodists of all time, could often concentrate on this motivic power to the exclusion of all other linear orders, and the melody is bypassed as we move from the motif directly to the largest aspects of musical form.

In Schoenberg's music before serialism, the relation of dissonance and consonance had so weakened as to be useless on a large scale and became concentrated in the motif. Harmonic dissonance almost disappeared, but it could be reconstructed by shape and texture—by the upward and downward curves of the motif, by the increasing or decreasing intensity of its rhythmic movement. Serialism then allowed an almost unlimited source of motivic variation with an assurance of the unity of all the successive developments from the same series.

Schoenberg based the expressivity of music on the shape and texture of the motif, but his view of serialism ignored precisely shape and texture. The freedom here was anarchic: the series could be realized at any point by a rising as well as by a falling interval, and rhythmic shape was also indifferent to the serial aspect. The neoclassical forms to which Berg and Schoenberg turned offered a semblance of order, but this demanded a renunciation of the motivic technique of *Erwartung* and the Five Pieces for Orchestra in favor of a thematic structure (as in Berg's *Lulu* and Schoenberg's violin and piano concertos, and third and fourth quartets). In short, neoclassicism required a mimesis of tonal melody. Only this way, it seemed, could rhythm and texture escape anarchy.

Of the three first serialists, Webern alone made a profound exploration of athematic forms, and he rarely experimented with a serialist version of tonal melody. In his search for order, however, he wrote music more rigidly symmetrical than any of Schoenberg's or Berg's, and largely confined himself to a limited version of serialism that would give him the absolute symmetries he needed, often using a series in which the second hexachord is an exact reflection of the first. His forms are as neoclassic as Schoenberg's, a serial analogue of the early-eighteenth-century binary dance form appearing ever more frequently. The rage for order in the 1920s was such that neatness and simplicity were frequently identified, not least by Webern, with intelligibility: one might almost assume that neither Webern's Six Pieces for Orchestra, opus 6, of 1909, nor Schoenberg's *Erwartung* were intelligible forms to the composers in their later years. An intelligible order for Webern meant, above all, an easily perceived equilibrium; from this came his penchant for minor forms, which provided a compromise between the old desire for the music never to repeat itself with the new longing for exact repetition. In some of Webern's works, the conjunction of a series with its retrograde amounts almost to an obsession.

Webern achieved a neoclassic style without an analogue of "tonal" melody at the cost of an almost exclusive concentration on segmented versions of the series. These segments are equivalent, in fact, to the motifs of nineteenth-century style. So intense was Webern's concentration on the motif that one may say that his motifs are not really derived from the series; they generate it. His String Quartet, opus 28, of 1938, has a row composed of the same motif repeated twice:

The motif is once more the famous B-A-C-H that we have met with before; such a series falls apart at once into its three motivic segments. To reveal relationships between versions of the motif, the rhythm of this quartet is relentlessly four-square: rhythmic nuances are left entirely to the *rubato* of the performer. As in Schoenberg the expressivity is derived chiefly from the motif, but the texture of Webern's String Quartet does not reinforce this: it remains transparent. The warmth of feeling in Webern is the performer's responsibility, and he insisted that it be brought out: played simply, his music has a cool grace as beautiful as the repressed and violent intensity that Webern intended one to hear.

Both Schoenberg's long melodies and Webern's fragmentation are attempts to circumvent serialism as much as they are efforts to exploit it; both composers tried at times to avoid considering the series as a unit. They wrote serial music to some extent as if it were constructed from single notes; that is, they were often more preoccupied with the relation of notes within the series than in the operation of the series taken as a whole. Even when Schoenberg explored the relation between two different versions of one series, it was generally to find a motivic form common to both, or to play with similarities between two hexachords.

But musical systems appear to have a life of their own, and they resist certain ways of exploiting them, seeming —by a kind of magnetic force—to pull in unpredictable directions. Once created, serialism imposed itself in ways that no one had foreseen.

The series has a rhythm of its own opposed to the classical forms in that it is periodic, constantly recurring. By this quality it transcends its inner organization. The periodicity is of an exceptional sort in that it is totally independent of pulsation, unrelated to a measurable tempo. Since different forms of the series in one work may overlap, and may be played with the different notes spaced out or grouped all at once in a chord, the period

may not be easily measurable as we normally understand that, but it is none the less invariable and consistent. It creates an invariance of its own that lies behind
what the composer is doing and of which he may not
always be fully conscious.

The periodic nature of serialism means, too, that the
fundamental unit of music composed in this form is not
the note but the series as a whole, a larger unit and
harder to grasp—for composer as well as listener. It is
difficult to hear in that it is not specifically correlated
with the actual duration of the notes: a direct correlation
(as one sometimes finds in Webern) is, in fact, partially
self-defeating, reducing the rhythm of the series to the
rhythm of the notes taken singly. This serial "rhythm"
has classical roots, as it is obviously related to (and even
derived from) the motivic structure of Beethoven, particularly late Beethoven, where the continuous recurrence of motifs throughout the texture does not always
coincide either with the pulse or with the harmonic
rhythm, although interlocking with both. The period of
a series, however, has a larger compass than that of a
motif, and, most important of all, it is total, involving
every note in a piece.

For this reason, once the periodicity of the series is
heard, it is not merely a contributing element to the
other kinds of rhythm, but overrides them all, just as the
rhythm of the succession of periodic phrases in Brahms
and Chopin, for example, regulates the nuances and the
rubatos within the individual measures. Since the periodicity of the series is independent of tempo and does not
conform to a regular unit, it makes the strict and regular
rhythms of the neoclassical period sound anachronistic,
and it can be heard through them as through a grid.

The rhythm of the successive realizations of the series

created a form that seemed at times to be antagonistic to the forms derived from tonality. There are works, however, in which Schoenberg, consciously or unconsciously, reckoned clearly with it and allowed it to shape the music as it proceeded: his insistence upon working at high speed and his extraordinary reliance upon instinct and inspiration made this natural. Most notable of these works are the Music for a Film Sequence, parts of *Moses und Aron,* and the String Trio in which he explicitly set out to portray his real death and reawakening. In these pieces the listener is perhaps most aware of the continuous background movement, as the series in its many forms is realized in an extraordinary variety of shapes and rhythms. It would perhaps have given Schoenberg himself an ironic pleasure to think that the works in which nonmusical feelings were most deeply involved were the ones for which he developed his most satisfying abstract forms.

SHORT BIBLIOGRAPHY

The most important discussion of Schoenberg's stylistic development is to be found in Jan Maegaard, *Studien zur Entwicklung des dodekaphonen Satzes bei Arnold Schönberg* (Copenhagen: Wilhelm Hansen, 1972). I unfortunately read this work only after my own manuscript had been finished, but have been able to add a footnote on page 39 concerning this extraordinarily detailed study.

Josef Rufer's catalogue of Schoenberg's works, *The Works of Arnold Schoenberg* (London: Faber & Faber, 1962), was invaluable, but has been partly superseded by Maegaard.

There is an excellent account of the available publications of Schoenberg's music in *Musical Newsletter,* IV, 3 (Summer 1974), written by David Hamilton. Schoenberg's music was published largely by Universal, Vienna, until 1932 (except for opus 23 and 24, published by Hansen, Copenhagen). After 1932, the main publisher was G. Schirmer in New York. Schoenberg's estate, which has taken over the copyright of many works, is directing the publication of a complete critical edition, published by Barenreiter, several volumes of which have already appeared.

Schoenberg's own critical prose writings are to be found in *Style and Idea,* trans. Dika Newlin, first published New York: Philosophical Library, 1950; a new, much enlarged edition is promised from Faber & Faber. Of his theoretical writings, the most important is the *Harmonielehre* of 1911, revised in 1921; 7th ed., 1966. The other theoretical writings are results of his teaching at UCLA and were compiled with the assistance of Leonard Stein. They are: *Structural Functions of Harmony,* rev. ed., New York: Norton, 1969, and *Preliminary Exercises in Counterpoint,* New York: St. Martin's Press, 1964. Schoenberg's *Letters,* ed. Stein, trans. Wilkins and Kaiser, is published by Faber & Faber, London, 1964. Interesting critical treatment of Schoenberg is to be found in the various articles in *Perspectives on Schoenberg and Stravinsky,* eds. B. Boretz and E. T. Cone, Princeton, N. J.: Princeton University Press, 1968; paper ed., New York: Norton, 1972. The fullest account of Schoenberg's life in English is to be found in Willi Reich, *Arnold Schoenberg: A Critical Biography,* trans. Leo Black, New York: Praeger, 1971, although it is anything but critical. The best treatment of twelve-tone technique remains George Perle's *Serial Composition and Atonality,* 2d ed., Berkeley, Calif.: University of California Press, 1969.

The bibliography in Maegaard's book is complete to 1972. A small list of important articles and books might include:

Berg, Alban. "Why Is Schoenberg's Music So Difficult?" in *Alban Berg* by Willi Reich, trans. Cornelius Cardew. New York: Harcourt Brace, 1965.

Boulez, Pierre, "Schoenberg est mort," in *Relevés d'apprenti.* Paris: Editions du Seuil, 1966.

Buchman, Herbert H. "A Key to Schoenberg's *Erwartung* (op. 17)," *Journal of the American Musicological Society,* XX, 3 (1967).

Friedham, Philip. "Rhythmic Structure in Schoenberg's Atonal Compositions," *Journal of the American Musicological Society,* XIX, 1 (1966).

Leibowitz, René. *Schoenberg and His School,* trans. Dika Newlin. New York: Da Capo Press, 1970.

Newlin, Dika. *Bruckner, Mahler and Schoenberg.* New York: King's Crown Press, 1947.

Stuckenschmidt, H. H. *Schoenberg,* trans. Searle and Temple-Roberts. London: Calder, 1959.

Webern, Anton von. *The Path to the New Music.* New York: Presser, 1963.

Wellescz, Egon. *Arnold Schoenberg,* trans. Kerridge. New York: Greenwood, 1925.

Whittall, Arnold, *Schoenberg Chamber Music.* London: BBC, 1972.

INDEX